# *Hidden* POWER

Tap into a kingdom

principle that will

change you forever

# TOMMY BARNETT

HIDDEN POWER by Tommy Barnett
Published by Charisma House
A part of Strang Communications Company
600 Rinehart Road
Lake Mary, Florida 32746
www.charismahouse.com

Unless otherwise noted, all Scripture quotations are from the Holy Bible, New International Version. Copyright © 1973, 1978, 1984, International Bible Society. Used by permission.

Scripture quotations marked KJV are from the King James Version of the Bible.

Cover design by Debbie Lewis

Library of Congress Catalog Card Number: 2002103067
International Standard Book Number: 0-88419-771-9

02 03 04 05 87654321
Printed in the United States of America

Dedicated to my pastoral staff and the board
of deacons of Phoenix First Assembly of God,
all godly leaders who exemplify the *Hidden
Power.* Each one of these dear friends has
caught the spirit of this book, allowing me to
live the *Hidden Power* principle, and they have
lived it out in their own lives also. I thank
God for their lives—to God be the glory for
these living examples of *Hidden Power.*

# CONTENTS

# FOREWORD

There are many different types of heroes. There are those who save lives. There are those who dream great dreams. There are those who have done what no one else has attempted. My pastor is my hero for all of these reasons. Tommy Barnett is known as a lifesaver and a restorer for the kingdom of God, a dreamer of great dreams and a courageous risk taker. He strives toward and accomplishes great things that no one else has done before. And although his heroics may not fit the mold, he is my hero and someone I admire for several reasons. These include his perseverance for the things of God and his devoted love for others.

Pastor Tommy Barnett is an incredible seeker and an incredible dreamer. He is always going after the goals and visions that God has for his life, always pursuing life to the fullest. Right now he is involved in many different projects, including what he calls *Vision 2000*, which is a project designed to provide buildings and facilities that will reach out to the surrounding community. That is his goal at Phoenix First Assembly—to reach out to the city and meet the needs of others. He is also incredible at what he does behind the pulpit. I love going to services where he is preaching and teaching, because he always has something great to say. He is always encouraging, but also challenging in what he says, driving the church and myself to seek deeper things in God. The reason I admire this so much in him is that he is one who actively applies the things he is preaching about. It's much like he's going on a journey and we're all joining with him in his journey. But we know that it's not just his journey, but God's journey for all of us. I know that he spends time with God and seeks Him constantly to receive the things he does. That is something that I admire very much in him.

His love for others is also an incredible gift. His desire is to see others succeed in God's plans for their lives, and he seeks to do all he can to help them. Many of his staff members have gone on to become great spiritual leaders and examples across the globe, and many others have remained and successfully live in their dreams. More that that, my pastor loves to see people "dream again." He and his son have pioneered the Los Angeles International Church, also known as the Dream Center, which is devoted to helping people in the inner city. They provide housing, job training, discipleship, food and hospital facilities to reach out directly to the needs of those who are often neglected. Many other churches are also creating Dream Centers around the world and modeling after the success of the Los Angeles Dream Center.

But the really incredible thing about him is that he may be the leader of many different things and a great pastor, but he always has time for people like me. I love it when I see him in the hallway and he gives me a smile or shakes my hand. I know that he may not know my name, but he is always inviting and always friendly, and I know he loves me. He will be the first to tell you that it's not his own love, but God's love in him that motivates all he does. And God's love flows out of him. He will tell you that it is because of what God has done in his life and that it is a gift—and indeed it is.

I want to be like my pastor, someone who dreams big and sees God work through his life in ways that only God can. I too want to strive after the greatest goal (which is not found in building big buildings or being a great leader). I want to be a servant, a lover of people, just like my pastor. I want to walk in God's plans for my life and to see His love central to everything I do, just like my pastor. I want to follow after Christ above all else and have a heart devoted only to Him, just like my pastor. After all, he is not only my pastor, he's my hero.[1]

—MARK KNOLES,
SEVENTEEN-YEAR-OLD MEMBER
OF PHOENIX FIRST ASSEMBLY

# INTRODUCTION

Unlock your imagination for a moment.

Picture yourself in a cabin in the woods. You're on a lovely vacation in the mountains, and one day you go out walking through a forest of pine trees. As you meander along, relaxing and enjoying the pure air, something on the ground catches your eye—a glint of metal among the pine needles. You stoop and brush away the needles, and to your astonishment, there in the ground is an electric outlet, right in the middle of the woods!

Amazed, you try to dig around it, but it's firmly buried, and there's no way to see where it leads. Overwhelmed with curiosity, you walk back to the cabin, a stone's throw away, and grab a small radio. You plug it in and music blares out.

You decide to run an extension cord from the strange outlet and see what else it can handle. To your amazement, everything you plug in works, and the outlet shows no sign of blowing a fuse or shorting out.

The power company says it doesn't know whom the outlet belongs to, and nobody is being billed for the power. You call your neighbors and tell them to plug in to the extension cord, and soon the mysterious outlet is lighting up the whole neighborhood.

Eventually the city catches on and builds a power plant directly on top of the outlet, and every resident enjoys free electricity. There's so much excess that the power company begins selling it to the rest of America, then giving it away, and electric bills become a thing of the past—all because you found this small, seemingly insignificant, easily overlooked outlet.

Anywhere the principle is applied, it provides unlimited power to establish God's kingdom on earth.

That's how I feel about the subject of this book. It is the single reason for whatever success God has given me. It is the "hidden" outlet that drives my ministry.

It is also, whether you know it or not, the reason for whatever success you have had at your work, in your friendships and long-term relationships, with your children and in your marriage. At times you have plugged in to this principle, maybe blindly, but when you did you could almost feel a jolt of power surging through you, and you realized it works.

Anywhere the principle is applied, it provides unlimited power to establish God's kingdom on earth. That's what it was designed to do. I'd like to show you how to plug in to it.

## IDEAS THAT WORK

I was seventeen when I left college and became a traveling evangelist. I'm sixty-four now and have been in the ministry for forty-seven years—through great years of growth and also periods of heartache. I have been part of, and now pastor, two of the largest churches in America. In other cities like Detroit and New York, men I personally trained pastor churches of the same size as mine.

The ideas we tried at our church have influenced churches throughout America. Our emphasis on soulwinning, reaching the poor, taking buses into the inner city and picking people up for church has changed the way churches interact with their communities.

The showy things we do—like Christmas and Easter pageants, Fourth of July extravaganzas and illustrated sermons—are now common parts of church life.

Even the programs that started in my church—like Master's Commission, the Dream Center and NAME, a marriage ministry—have spread literally around the world.

What excites me about all this is that we found ideas that work, and others are blessed by them also.

All of the good ideas have worked because of

the single underlying principle we'll talk about in this book. In a way, this book is the sum of my thoughts about what works in the Christian life and what doesn't. I have gone through the same questions and struggles every Christian goes through, wrestling late into the night or in hours of prayer. Now after all these years of observation and experience, I can distill my knowledge of what works into a single idea. I want to share it with you, because it offers unparalleled blessing and power.

I WANT THE POWER AND
BLESSING OF GOD TO
BE DIRECTED THROUGH
US AS BELIEVERS SO THAT
THE PLAN AND PURPOSE
OF GOD—HIS KINGDOM—
CAN TAKE ROOT HERE ON EARTH.

More importantly, I want the power and blessing of God to be directed through us as believers so that the plan and purpose of God— His kingdom—can take root here on earth. That's the real motive behind this book.

This book is about how I have tried to live my life and what works generally in ministry and in life. I want to share my "secret," if you can call it that. It's the most powerful idea I have found on the earth.

And it can change your life.

# ONE

# A
# NEW
# PARADIGM

I was surprised to see George W. Bush, then governor of Texas, come alone through the door into the room where my son Matthew and I were sitting. He extended his hand.

"Hi, I'm George Bush. Nice to meet you."

Matthew and I stood to shake his hand, and then we settled into our chairs for a few moments of introduction before the presidential candidate toured the Dream Center with us.

Moments earlier when Matthew and I were waiting for him, I had pictured what it would be like to meet Bush now that he was running for president. I was sure he would be surrounded by handlers and advisors, each pushing important papers before his eyes or whispering messages into his ears. I thought that he would be distracted by weighty matters, thoughts of strategy or responses to his rivals' accusations.

But I had been caught off guard when he made his entrance without the expected fanfare.

I noticed that he seemed unusually relaxed for a man in his position. He looked us in the eye as he spoke, apparently not distracted by the constant mental noise of a campaign. He was gentle, warm and friendly as we spoke about our work in Los Angeles.

Once again, I marveled that he was here at all.

## Bouncing Back

Less than forty-eight hours earlier Bush had lost an important primary election in Michigan and was facing turmoil within his political party and in the media at large. Columnists were wondering if he could bounce back, if he had the will to fight. They questioned his inner fortitude, his stamina, his ability to slug it out. It even looked as if he might lose the nomination to another candidate who had more momentum.

From where did he draw strength? What motivated him? How did he make important decisions?

Now, in the middle of the whirlwind of politics and media coverage, I was getting a glimpse of him at one of his most critical hours. He was visiting us at the Dream Center and was going to make a major policy speech there, but he seemed anything but rattled. If I had suffered a somewhat humiliating loss, I would have wanted to crawl in a hole for a while, but Bush didn't appear to be bothered.

As we got acquainted I wondered what kind of man he was. From where did he draw strength? What motivated him? How did he make important decisions? Aside from his political viewpoints, what was he like as a man?

It wasn't my first time to meet him. Several months earlier in Dallas we were together at a meeting of pastors to which I had been invited by my friend James Robison. Men like Tony Evans, T. D. Jakes and Ed Young Jr. were there. At the time, Bush was still weighing his decision to run, and that day he shared the fears he had about what might happen to his family—and especially his daughters—in the poison spotlight of politics. He talked about his conversion. That day we prayed that whatever decision Bush made, God would protect him and his family. After our time together, I invited him to the Dream Center, and he politely said he would come.

I didn't figure he actually would, considering his busy campaign schedule. I'm sure he received hundreds of invitations, and yet one day the phone rang at the Dream Center. It was his campaign staff. They gave us three days' notice that they wished to visit. On the day he arrived at around 1 A.M. in the morning, Matthew had busloads of people at the airport to greet him with welcome signs and cheers—a particularly meaningful gesture considering his loss in Michigan.

Now here I was, sitting across from him in a room at the Dream Center. It was a moment I knew could be fashioned only by God. We had never lobbied for political influence. We served the poor in one of the poorest districts of Los Angeles. For whatever reason, God had put us together, at least for that day, with a soon-to-be world leader who would lead the United States during one of our most crucial times in history.

We took Bush to see the children in our private school. He listened to their presentation and was clearly moved by the sight of these poor kids getting an education in a safe environment. He told them a story and had his picture taken with them; then he gave them a pep talk about going on to get their education so they could amount to something outstanding.

## CHRIST AND THE REPORTERS

From there we went into the auditorium where big Dream Center signs hung behind a long table at which he, myself and Matthew sat. By that time he was joined by his advisors and the ever-present Texas Rangers who monitored his every move. They had scouted out the place thoroughly and were positioned around the campus, from the ground floor to the roof.

The auditorium was filled with reporters and television cameras. We packed the place every week for our Sunday and Thursday services, but probably never with so many gatekeepers of public opinion. All the major reporters from the networks, along with their camera crews, were present, pens ready, lenses trained on us. Matthew and I took the podium and told the media about the Dream Center. At Bush's request we introduced three people to give them an idea of what the Dream Center was all about.

First was Donna, a black woman in her forties, who had been in prison several times. She was a serious criminal, but she had turned her life around and gone through our discipleship program. Now she is on our paid staff. She spoke of how people had given up on her throughout all of her life. She had lost her children, but now she had them back. Her daughter attends a major college in Los Angeles.

As she spoke, Bush interrupted to ask if anyone else in her family had been to college, and she said no. He was so moved that he asked her to send him an invitation to her daughter's graduation and said that he would try to come. (Now she writes him frequently, and he writes back. She was even invited to the inauguration.)

Billy Soto was next. He once played for the Little Anthony rock band, but because of his thirty-year drug addiction he had lost his wife and children. But he met the Lord, straightened out his life and got his family back. He has been at the Dream Center for six years and now heads up the Under the Bridge ministry to homeless people. During our services he's on stage playing guitar. He told how his life had been wrecked, but Christ restored it. By the time he finished, the big-shot reporters' mouths were agape!

Then there was José, once a gang member in Oakland. He had served prison time. He had been ensnared by drugs, but got out of prison, got saved and came to the Dream Center. He now pastors our Spanish church.

After the three testimonies, which had quieted the room, an amazing thing happened. Bush took the podium. Matthew and I were sitting right behind him.

"I know you don't understand what these people are talking about," Bush said to the gathering. "To understand, you have to experience it. I have experienced it. If I become president, I'm going to see that money goes to faith-based organizations like this because they get the job done."

He went on to give his prepared speech, and I was gratified that he would publicly acknowledge his faith in Christ. The non-Christians in the building that day surely felt the power of his words and of the true stories of God's grace that had come before.

After his speech he took a break before holding a press conference. During the break I was present for an impromptu strategy meeting held concerning something one of the other candidates was saying. I was very flattered that he trusted me to be there.

The next day a photograph of Bush and me appeared on the front page of *The New York Times*. A year later *The New York Times* sent another reporter over and did a major article about the Dream Center, with a photo on the front page and a headline that read: "Praised by Bush, a Church Center From the Streets!" The article went on to state: "When George W. Bush was campaigning for president, he stopped in downtown Los Angeles at the Dream Center and praised it as the kind of religious antipoverty program he wants to support."[1]

I was reminded again that you cannot orchestrate those kinds of things. The future president visiting your church...front-page coverage on *The New York Times*...a major follow-up a few months later. Somehow, as we had reached down to the poorest, most forgotten folks in society, God had raised us up to the heights.

## A LOOK IN THE EYE

Years earlier I had the privilege of introducing Ronald Reagan at a banquet in Iowa when he was campaigning for the Republican nomination. I sat right next to him as we ate, and as we talked I felt as though I were the only person in the room. He looked at me with that Reaganesque teary look, very sympathetic, nodding his head when I spoke. He gave all his attention to one person at a time. Other people of his stature would look over your shoulder and wave to other people when they spoke with you, but not him. He looked in my eyes and listened. I told my wife later that night, "If people can look in Reagan's eyes and see what I saw—that kind, gentle love—he'll be president." Television picked that up and conveyed it to millions, and he was indeed elected.

When I met Bush, I felt he was the same kind of man. He looked you right in the eye. He was kind, not a hotshot. He gave you time and attention. After the event he stood around and shook hands with everyone and was in no hurry to leave. (Later, after he became president, people began to note that after major speeches in the Capitol he shakes hands with the congressional pages rather than wave at them from behind the velvet ropes. Some of the pages have choked up because they've been so moved.)

I'm not familiar enough with George Bush personally to know about his spiritual history, though I have read and heard him testify of his own faith in Christ. I'm not pushing support for any particular policy or party. I tell that story because it shows the kinds of blessings that come when we follow the kingdom way, reaching out to others, giving ourselves to the poor. It's a way of living that may seem paradoxical, yet it brings many blessings.

## GOING BACKWARDS ON PURPOSE

If you're like me, your life is spent looking for answers: How do I live a life that matters? If the Christ-life is so revolutionary, how do I make it work for me?

If you're like me, you struggle with issues of obedience, surrender, love and a host of doctrinal questions that keep me digging into the Word. I've always been hungry for the truth, even if it put me at odds with men. I want to know God, and I want to work with Him effectively.

Sometimes during life we may get sidetracked into doctrinal arguments or get caught up in churches or groups that emphasize certain teachings, but the sincere person bounces back to center and rediscovers the basic things that make the gospel so wonderful, so mysterious, so full of energy and answers.

So what does the gospel teach? What is its essence? If you think about it, the basic teaching of the gospel is the kingdom of God and how to live and move within it. Jesus spent most of His time talking about the kingdom and demonstrating it. To Him it was a real thing that had consequences in this life and in the next.

> GOD'S KINGDOM OPERATES
> UPSIDE DOWN AND BACKWARDS
> FROM THE NATURAL KINGDOM.

That's really what this book is about. It's about the kingdom and how you can embrace, experience and extend it in your own world—not tomorrow or in the "sweet by and by," but today, right now.

The most important thing to know about the kingdom is this: God's kingdom operates upside down and backwards from the natural kingdom.

If you don't understand that principle, you will always be confused. Most people, even unbelievers, know deep inside that we live in two worlds, the natural realm and the spiritual realm, simultaneously.

But it's not good enough to know that we are spiritual beings. We have to cooperate with God in His plan for humanity. As believers, we live simultaneously in the kingdom realm and in the natural realm, and the two pull us in opposing directions. Why? It is because the kingdom of light sometimes bears no resemblance to the natural realm. The natural realm might tell us to invest here, move there, say this or do that—but the kingdom message we get in our spirits tells us to do the opposite.

That's why Jesus said repeatedly in His Sermon on the Mount:

> You have heard that it was said...but I tell you...
>
> —MATTHEW 5:21–22

He was correcting decades and centuries of natural thinking, which had crusted over kingdom truths like barnacles on the hull of a ship. Jesus knew the kingdom perfectly, and He spent enormous amounts of time telling people how the kingdom worked, convincing them, encouraging them, getting them to listen to the Holy Spirit rather than to their natural thoughts.

You see, the kingdom way is not innately understood. If it were, Jesus would not have needed to speak His words, and we would not need the Gospels. We would only need our intuition, hunches and common sense. If, as some man-centered religions say, we only need to look inside ourselves for answers, then the world would already be a better place and we wouldn't need God. But that hasn't happened. The world is sick, and God is its only cure.

Kingdom principles come from the Holy Spirit, who conveys them to our hearts and plants them like seeds to grow in the soil of our understanding. When we tend to them by practicing them, the seeds grow, and we learn to move with the moves of God.

The apostle Paul knew this. If he had a single theme it might be renewal of the mind—another way of saying we need to plug in to the new reality instead of the old, the *kingdom way* instead of the *natural way*.

> ## THE WORLD IS SICK, AND GOD IS ITS ONLY CURE.

This old realm is running out of power. In fact, the power has already been spent. Natural principles can't keep the world running. But the kingdom is everlasting, ever-increasing, ever-expanding. It's the future. It's what we need to fulfill our individual purposes.

And at the center of it all is the principle of this book, which I'm going to share with you. But I want to lay this groundwork so you see why it works. Otherwise it might seem like a gimmick. To fully grasp this principle you must be ready to go backward.

## REVERSE GEAR

It's actually more productive to go backward than forward. What do I mean? I mean that the people who go in full reversal of what this world thinks ultimately receive more honor than those who go forward.

So many men and women are racing, competing to do something meaningful, but how many actually do it? The trick is not outrunning everyone, but going in the opposite direction.

Think of Gandhi. He did the upside-down thing. Everyone else said force and power and war were the right ways, but he thought backwards. He said nonviolence was more powerful, and he proved it. To this day, India and the world live in the shadow of his example.

Why is he such a hero? Because he went backward faster than anyone else in his day.

Think of Mother Teresa. Yes, we all know of her work among the destitute and dying. We've all seen the pictures showing her eyes exuding compassion. She is the closest thing the world has to a universal saint. Yet it's useful to remember that Agnes Gonxha Bojaxhiu was born a person like you and me. (In 1931 Mother Teresa took the name of Teresa from the French nun Thérèse Martin, who was canonized in 1927 with the title St. Thérèse of Lisieux.)[2] She would have lived a normal life and died with a one-inch obituary like anyone else if she hadn't chosen to do things backwards and upside down.

The shortcut to greatness is found in reverse gear. In an automobile, reverse is the slowest and most awkward gear, but in the kingdom, it's the secret weapon. It has rocket boosters on it and a guidance system. It takes you further and faster.

Did it make sense that future President Bush would visit a place where the least of society are honored? Not necessarily. Natural thinking says that men of power occupy the halls of power and insulate themselves from others—especially the down and dirty. But God's way works. I may never have met George W. Bush if I had devoted myself to currying favor with men. But when we did what God asked of us, He rewarded us with a wonderful day with the future president.

THE SHORTCUT
TO GREATNESS IS
FOUND IN REVERSE GEAR.

Though the point of doing the kingdom thing is not to gain honor or influence on earth, that will happen. You may not be recognized in your day, but everyone who lives the kingdom way will get every measure of honor they have earned.

People think I have been blessed because I have a lot of energy or love people, but in truth I have only as much energy as the next man, and I haven't always loved people as I do now.

The secret, if you can call it that, is that the kingdom way is the backward way. I try the kingdom way first.

> But seek first his kingdom and his righteousness, and all these things will be given to you as well.
> —MATTHEW 6:33

Seeking the kingdom doesn't always mean praying in a dark closet. It means seeking, in a very practical way, the kingdom-minded solution in any situation.

> In all your ways acknowledge him, and he will make your paths straight.
> —PROVERBS 3:6

What does it mean to "acknowledge him"? What is God telling you? What is the kingdom thing He is asking you to do right now? Does He want you to...

- Take another job?
- Tell your spouse you love him or her?
- Go back to college?
- Start a new ministry?

The kingdom way means doing the thing that is fearful. That believes in plenty, not lack. It's doing the brave thing and doing it with confidence. The kingdom way means doing the thing that scares you, but which your spirit tells you is right.

## THE LIGHTS OF GLORY

As I get older I sometimes imagine that I'm able to glimpse the lights of glory in the promised land. Sometimes I even want to go there. Like everyone who lives long enough, I realize I won't be here forever, and at times I wonder if I have contributed anything worthwhile to this old world. Do I stand among the brave and faithful? How will my service to God be judged?

Of this I am sure: The principle we discuss in this book is the root of any effective work that I have been part of. It begins with realizing that the kingdom works upside down and backwards.

Each chapter of this book is specially crafted to show you how to improve your relationship with God and others, to make you a super-effective Christian by doing the upside-down thing—the backward thing. It's sometimes going in the opposite direction of what good old-fashioned "horse sense" may tell you to do.

THE KINGDOM WAY
MEANS DOING THE THING
THAT SCARES YOU, BUT WHICH
YOUR SPIRIT TELLS YOU IS RIGHT.

Now that we know we have to do the upside-down thing to achieve what God wants for us, I want to share what I believe is the defining principle that has allowed my ministry to be effective for God. We'll see what it is in the next chapter.

# Two

# Giving
# in Order
# to Receive

I stood in the sanctuary of the empty Angelus
Temple, the famous church built by Foursquare
founder Aimee Semple McPherson, and found
myself close to tears. I looked up at the slate-blue
dome directly overhead. It was well lit and
resplendent, though the rest of the sanctuary was
dim. The mural of a resurrected Jesus behind the
platform still inspired awe, and the stained-glass
windows two stories high gave the feel of a
modern cathedral.

But this was no ordinary cathedral. For years,
the innovative Sister Aimee had used this as her
pulpit to the world. In the 1930s she was more
famous than any film or music star. Thousands
flocked every Sunday to hear her preach and to
see her many spectacles, illustrated sermons,
great choirs and dramatic presentations.

Most of all they came because she loved them.
She wasn't just putting on a show. She was

feeding the hungry—one and a half million of them during the Great Depression.

She was giving people hope during hard times.

She was delivering the gospel to a city desperate for a true message among the glitter of movies.

Trolley cars used to line up outside on Sunday evenings just to take the people home. And as they rode through those darkened streets, still humming tunes from the service, people would think, *The world may be a dark place, but there's always Angelus Temple. I know they love me there.*

## SHE WAS GIVING PEOPLE HOPE DURING HARD TIMES.

But in recent decades the church had dwindled in size and influence. It still held a special place in the hearts of Foursquare and Pentecostal believers everywhere, but it wasn't having the impact it used to have. No buses lined up to take people to and from church. There were no illustrated sermons or grand special days. The place had been designated a national historical landmark, and it was beginning to act that way.

But that was all about to change...

## A HERO OF MINE

My ministry has been greatly influenced by three people: a Baptist preacher named Jack Hyles, Aimee Semple McPherson and my father. When I was young I read about Aimee's life and listened to people who had seen her minister. I decided that there were three things about her ministry that I wanted to emulate:

- I wanted to make soulwinning the number one priority of my ministry.
- I wanted to heal people's hurts.
- I wanted to use big events and the arts to reach people.

I felt a kinship with Aimee. I liked the bigness of the vision in her heart because I too felt drawn to do big things for God. Using the same principles I saw at work in her life, I put on illustrated sermons, held huge Easter and Christmas pageants and big Fourth of July fireworks shows, each drawing tens of thousands of people. We used laser light shows, live animals, singing Christmas trees, flying angels and anything else we could imagine. We attracted as many as thirty thousand people to one performance.

When my church, Phoenix First Assembly, built a new sanctuary—at the time the largest church sanctuary in the country—it had two balconies, just like Angelus Temple.

Then there were our outreaches to the poor. I had started busing people to the church when I pastored in Davenport (something Aimee didn't do), and I continued to do it in Phoenix. Every Sunday, more than forty buses collected our congregants who lived in the poor parts of town. Children, the handicapped, the jobless, the hopeless—our bus drivers invited them on, loved them and took them to our church where they were welcomed with open arms.

When my son Matthew and I started the

Dream Center in Los Angeles, our entire focus was on reaching the impoverished. The Dream Center started in one of the most godless, crime-ridden neighborhoods in the United States. Unlike in Aimee's day, it was not a place for the affluent to live—it was an inner-city, bars-on-the-windows kind of place. Those were our surroundings, and those were the people we were determined to reach. We took buses to the original Skid Row and even rounded up the homeless men from under the bridges. Soon we were reaching thousands every week.

I did it because I knew it was right and because Jesus had commanded it. But I had the faith to do it because I knew it had been done before by Sister Aimee. Many people told us it couldn't be done in that crime-filled area. Sometimes in the face of a challenge or opportunity I would tell myself, "If Aimee could do it, so can I."

## "SOMEDAY..."

Now I stood in her church, a lump in my throat, a swell of gratitude in my heart. The impossible had happened—Angelus Temple was uniting with the Dream Center to reach Los Angeles, and Matthew was ordained as its pastor.

The Temple and the Dream Center, two great landmarks sitting only six blocks apart, would be twin engines of revival in Los Angeles, with the Temple once again becoming a great soulwinning church and the Dream Center continuing to grow as a huge discipleship and outreach center. We believed that with the partnership of these two ministries, we could reach one hundred thousand people every week.

I started to walk out of the Temple amid workers in hard hats who were busy drilling under the balcony with jackhammers to make room for more seats. New seats would bring the seating capacity to nearly four thousand. Piles of dirt and concrete littered the ground floor, and all the seats had been removed to make room for new theater seats. The two balconies curved majestically overhead.

> SOMETIMES IN THE FACE OF A
> CHALLENGE OR OPPORTUNITY
> I WOULD TELL MYSELF, "IF
> AIMEE COULD DO IT, SO CAN I."

The beat of the workmen's equipment was music to my ears; I knew that in a few months it would give way to the music of praise filling this place once again. With the help of God we were going to kick-start that church that virtually had been closed down and draw the hurting people in from the inner city. Aimee would be proud of the needy, hurting crowd that would come.

It was one of the greatest experiences of my life, but it wasn't entirely unexpected. At the age of nineteen, I had an experience I had never really told anyone about—one that portended it.

As a young, nineteen-year-old preacher, I was preaching a revival at Bethel Temple in Los Angeles, which at the time was an affluent church. Bethel Temple was one of the first churches born out of the Azusa Street revival. (It also was the first church Matthew and I used when we came to Los Angeles to start the Dream Center. By that time Bethel Temple had shrunk to a congregation of less than fifty. After a year in that location, we moved the congregation to the Queen of Angels hospital, which was where it became known as the Dream Center.)

## "YOU ARE GOING TO BE PART OF THAT CHURCH SOMEDAY."

That morning long ago as I drove to Bethel Temple to preach, I was listening to a Christian radio station as Ralph Carmichael directed one of his orchestras. It was a sunny day and the revival was going well, so I was pleased and content. My driving path happened to take me by Angelus Temple, located just a few blocks from Bethel Temple. I took a moment to admire the building as I drove by. As I did, something spoke to my heart: "You are going to be part of that church someday."

I immediately thought, *It can never happen. I'm an Assembly of God man. This is a Foursquare church.* But the impression was grafted deep into my soul.

I puzzled over it and locked it away in my heart, but I never forgot it. I had no way of making such a thing happen. Even if I wanted to do so, I had no inkling of how to do it. I decided that if God had spoken it, He could do it without my help. It was a thing of wonder to me—but something I would never dare to share publicly.

Now that it was happening, I knew God was fulfilling that promise of long ago. But I couldn't help but wonder why the Foursquare leaders would so readily turn it over to Matthew and me. What was the connection?

I asked them about it one day, and they told me they entrusted it to us because we were givers. Like Aimee, we gave our lives to the poor. Our whole lives revolved around healing hurts and winning lost souls. We spent huge amounts of effort and money to feed the hungry, clothe the naked, train the jobless, house the homeless and comfort the dying. Of all the paths we could have chosen in life, we chose the one of giving. It's what made us happiest.

That made them excited about putting us in charge of their most visible and prized church—the cornerstone and inspiration for the whole movement. Matthew and I were honored. Indeed, it's one of the great honors of our lives. More than that, we knew it was another opportunity to put this principle in action and give ourselves away.

## THE SECRET

Are you ready for the secret? Here it is. The secret to a successful, happy life is giving yourself away. According to the Bible, you will succeed in direct proportion to how much you give yourself away—and not just in ministry, but in marriage, raising your children, your friendships, your business, even your recreation.

I know it doesn't make sense. By nature we would rather possess than share, have than give. But if you follow the Lord long enough, one day it clicks: Joy is not living palms up—it's living palms down. Nobody has become happy from what they possessed, but anyone can increase their happiness by giving.

## THE SECRET TO A SUCCESSFUL, HAPPY LIFE IS GIVING YOURSELF AWAY.

Giving is truly the key to blessing. I have seen more souls saved in the last four years of my ministry than in the forty-seven years before. I have seen more money come through my hands for the ministry recently than ever before. Why? Not just because I have better staff or a better strategy than ever, but because we have learned to focus more and more on servanthood, downward mobility, on giving everything away.

We have found that the more we give away, the more God pours resources and surprise blessings into our hands.

Do you really believe it's better to give than to receive? Does the thought frighten you? In their minds, most Christians believe this principle works—but few actually practice it. Some see this tidbit of wisdom merely as a nice suggestion, never realizing the seismic power it holds.

I admit, it's not easy to convince yourself that the Bible and *only the Bible* is right. When it says, "It is more blessed to give than to receive," we should accept that as 100 percent correct—but often we don't (Acts 20:35). When it says, "The greatest among you will be your servant. For whoever exalts himself will be humbled, and whoever humbles himself will be exalted," we should accept it as a rock-solid fact—and act on it (Matt. 23:11–12). That's the stuff of revolutions.

But most people never reach that place in their lives.

## LACK VS. PLENTY

Why do we struggle with the principle of giving? A major hindering factor is the world in which we live—it encourages us to hold tightly to everything we have. Things always seem to be running out. Our cell phones have limited minutes and limited calling areas. Our cars can hold only so much gas. Our vacation time runs out. So does our patience, our energy, our attention. Our monthly budget seems to disappear down rabbit holes.

On a global scale we are told that the oil supply will run out in a few decades and that there isn't enough room on the planet for all the people who will be born. Some say the supply of fresh water is dwindling; others say that the ozone layer is thinning too quickly.

We are conditioned to think in terms of limits, and therefore the world operates on the principle of lack. The world says you start from a position of not having anything, and you have to grab and claw your way to a place of having enough. In the world, the successful man is the one who stores up the most—the million-dollar bank account, the 401K, the homes, the jet skis, the surround-sound entertainment system.

God approaches life from the opposite angle. He operates on the principle of plenty. In God's kingdom, the successful man or woman is the one who gives the most away.

The world says, "He who dies with the most toys wins." The kingdom says, "He who gives away the most wins."

God doesn't see the cup as half full or half empty—He sees it overflowing!

From God's perspective, words like *scarce resources, conserve, save up* and *limited* are meaningless. His is a world without limits, and we can connect to it.

THE WORLD SAYS, "HE
WHO DIES WITH THE MOST TOYS
WINS." THE KINGDOM SAYS, "HE
WHO GIVES AWAY THE MOST WINS."

I'm reminded of the Air Force fighter planes that fuel up while flying. A tanker flies right above the fighter and extends a gas pipeline down to the fighter's tank. The fighter doesn't have to land. It is refueled in midflight. That's what God does for us.

Our minds are juxtaposed between a world that says lack is the rule and a God who says we lack nothing. Our challenge is to act based on God's truth. We can demonstrate that by giving away as much as we can.

## STRIVING FOR GOOD THINGS?

Most Christians I know are sincere about wanting to please God, yet many of them are frustrated and end up striving toward God's promises.

There are plenty of books and teaching tapes about how to have more peace or joy or good relationships. In a way, that advice can encourage the kind of chasing after worldly things that God prohibits us from doing. Yes, we may be chasing the right things, but it may be done in the wrong spirit—a spirit of striving and worry.

Sad to say, I believe Christian books can take advantage of this by "selling" solutions— blessings, joy and peace—as if they can be chased down and grabbed. The advice tastes good, like ice cream on the tongue, and of course it's coated in Bible verses. But by the time it reaches our stomach there's nothing there, and the striving makes us ill.

Such striving encourages us to believe that we lack something. It clouds the fact that we already possess the promises of God. In fact, God's promises don't need to be hunted down. He has given them to us already! The secret, I believe, is realizing that in the kingdom life *there is no such thing as want*. In Christ, we have all that we need right now. We don't need books or teachings to bring us closer to the promises.

I have always said that happiness is not someone with whom you can start a relationship directly. You can't see him at a restaurant and introduce yourself. But if you introduce him to someone else, he'll turn to you and say, "You're the one I want to meet." That's how happiness enters our hearts.

Many believers think that in Christ *potentially* we have everything we need. But we can only access everything we need if we pray hard enough, read the right books or learn the right spiritual formulas.

IN THE KINGDOM
LIFE THERE IS NO
SUCH THING AS WANT.

Such a belief arises from a *lack mentality*. In truth, whether we are poor or rich ("whether living in plenty or in want" according to Paul in Philippians 4:12), we have everything we need. That means everything—from spiritual things to material things. For that reason Paul could say, "I am not saying this because I am in need, for I have learned to be content whatever the circumstances" (v. 11). He didn't chase down what he wanted. He knew he possessed it already in Christ.

Beloved, there is no need to search all over for the latest *key* to God's benefits. As a believer, even as you read these words you possess the promises. God can't make His Word any truer. It's up to you to flip the switch from unbelief to belief.

When we flip the switch we discover that we don't need to chase after the same things the rest of the world chases after—money or position, personal fulfillment or tranquility. To run after those things—or even after the things God wants us to have—is the first sign that we don't really have them. When we really believe we already have them, we can relax.

That, in turn, makes us better givers.

## THE SMILE MILE

When we know we have everything we need, we can gladly unlock the resources of our own hearts, bank accounts or schedules and give them away. The only godly response to a world where every miser, businessman, homemaker and child demands things of you is to give. Give even before someone has the chance to take from you. Go out of your way to give. Jesus said, "Give to the one who asks you, and do not turn away from the one who wants to borrow from you" (Matt. 5:42).

Life is going to take from you one way or another. Why not beat it to the punch and give? Jesus said:

> And if someone wants to sue you and take your tunic, let him have your cloak as well. If someone forces you to go one mile, go with him two miles... If you love those who love you, what reward will you get? Are not even the tax collectors doing that? And if you greet only your brothers, what are you doing more than others? Do not even pagans do that? Be perfect, therefore, as your heavenly Father is perfect.
> —MATTHEW 5:40–41, 46–48

Jesus said that any pagan can go one mile. It's easy to love those who love us. But we are not legalists who do as little as is required. As people of unlimited supply, we should go the second mile—the smile mile.

The smile mile is freely given, not demanded. It says to the taker, "I operate by different principles. You can demand something of me, and I'll always have more."

Jesus walked the smile mile when He forgave His enemies as He hung on the cross.

Paul sang as he walked it in the dungeon of a Roman jail.

> AS PEOPLE OF UNLIMITED SUPPLY, WE SHOULD GO THE SECOND MILE—THE SMILE MILE.

Any Christian who blesses those who curse him has taken steps along the smile mile.

Day after day as a little boy attended school, his lunch was stolen by a bully. The little boy was upset. One day he told his mother, and she made an extra lunch for the bully. That day, before the bully could demand his lunch, the boy handed him a brown paper bag. Stunned, the bully began to cry. No one had ever been kind to him before. He sat down next to the boy to eat his lunch, and they began to talk and laugh. Soon they were fast friends.

The *smile mile* had infected them both!

## BEING A GOOD SEED

Jesus pointed us to the seed that springs to life only when it has been buried in the dirt. He could have used any example from nature to explain His teaching. He might have said, "Be strong like the lion," or "Soar like the eagle." Instead, He drew His listeners' attention to something unexpected, apparently insignificant—like the principle we're talking about.

He said the seed shows us how to live. Is there anything less active than a seed? It just sits there! In order to be useful it must be buried. But the seed also holds the secret of giving.

Can you imagine trying to explain this idea to Fortune 500 industry leaders? You walk into a corporate boardroom to share the most profound secret of success, look these million-dollar men and women in the eye and say, "To succeed, you have to accept total defeat, death and burial—just like the seed."

Their stares would display their disbelieving thoughts. Soon they would tell you, "Quit wasting our time. Give us the latest business bestseller, not these bizarre ideas."

Yet the most successful Man who ever lived said, "Don't look at the thing that appears powerful. Look at the seed, and learn."

Let your imagination roam again, and picture with me a congregation of seeds—not just any seeds, but talking, walking, reasoning seeds. Seeds with little minds and little hands. This bunch of seeds finds itself on the side of a road near a big field. One of the seeds in the bunch looks around and says, "Fellas, I'm seeing a lot of potential here. Let's band together, start a business and build something big and meaningful." And that's what they do. They pool their ideas, energy and hard work, and they build something that resembles a tree.

That is, all except one seed. This seed has wisdom on its side, so it says to the other seeds, "I've thought about it, and I think there's a better way. God told us to soak up the sunshine and the water. He promised that something good would come out of it—even if we don't know exactly what. Let's bury ourselves and do our *work* in the soil." The others, intent upon making their mark on the world, ridicule the lonely seed.

But the little seed does the right thing and digs into the ground. Soon a different kind of work starts happening. While the other seeds cut down stalks of straw and try to build a large and imposing structure (which really looks like a sad, squashed bale of hay), the buried seed starts to feel energy churning inside of him. Something is coming to life.

The others mock him, even setting up a gravestone to mark his burial. It appears that he has wasted his life.

Eventually, the other seeds shrivel up in the sun. Their handmade structure outlasts them by a few weeks; then it falls apart in the rain. But that same rain is working a miracle under the ground as the little seed's energy bursts forth in a sprout of green. Soon it becomes a twig, then a trunk, and finally a huge tree bearing fruit that contains hundreds of other seeds.

See yourself as one of those seeds. Maybe you're an acorn or a pine nut. You have little arms and legs and a mind that can reason. What choice would you make?

What choice *do* you make?

LIFE ONLY WORKS
WHEN LIVED UPSIDE DOWN—
WHICH IS THE KINGDOM WAY.

Are you the one who gives his energy to building a reputation or a monument to your own ideas? Or do you give yourself away as God said to do?

Life only works when lived upside down—which is the kingdom way. It only works when lived backward from what you would naturally expect. Giving yourself away is not just a nice thought—it's an actual fact. It's like saying that internal combustion makes gasoline engines work. Giving is actually better than receiving—whether we like it or not. God made His kingdom to work that way, and if we don't play by His rules, we won't get His results.

I have found that when I plan or preach or pray without a giving spirit, my investment comes back small. But when I go into it by giving all the energy and fervency I have, I find myself replenished, and the investment multiplies immeasurably. That's how the "kingdom engine" works. You are free to put in it whatever you want, but the only way to get it to run effectively is to fill it with giving.

This principle of giving yourself away is more powerful than any automobile engine. It's even more powerful than an energy plant or booster rockets. It doesn't move just tons of steel—it moves mountains. It shapes destinies, sets the course of history, defines how governments and societies behave, inspires inventions. Literally, it is a force that no man can stop. Indeed, maybe giving is the one thing nobody can stop you from doing. Even if you were shackled and imprisoned, you could still give yourself away.

## ONLY WHAT YOU HAVE

We can only give what we have in our hearts. If you have worry, you give worry. Maybe you're the kind of person who worries about money, and now you're breeding that worry in your children or spouse.

> WHEN YOU TRULY HAVE THE PEACE
> OF GOD, IT SPREADS TO OTHERS
> LIKE A BEAUTIFUL FRAGRANCE.

If you have anger, you give anger. Maybe you blow up when things don't go as planned. Proverbs 19:3 says, "A man's own folly ruins his life, yet his heart rages against the LORD." In other words, an angry person ruins his own life and then blames God for the results.

But when you truly have the peace of God, it spreads to others like a beautiful fragrance. I have found that the most tranquil, faith-filled, happy people are those who give of themselves at every opportunity. They have risen to that heavenly level where nothing can make them stop giving.

## THREE LEVELS OF GIVING

There are three levels of living and giving.

### 1. THE HELLISH LEVEL

There is the hellish level where people return evil for good. When the Jewish leaders put Jesus to death and treated Him shamefully, they were acting on this hellish level. We see glimpses of this in our day when acts of kindness are paid back with evil. Examples of this level are seen when someone stops to help a stranded car and is assaulted, or when a personal relationship is betrayed after years of fidelity.

### 2. THE HUMAN LEVEL

Then there is the human level where people return good for good and evil for evil. The definition of most people's idea of morality most likely is this: an eye for an eye, and a tooth for a tooth. If you're nice to me, I'll be nice to you, but if you're mean to me, I'll be mean to you. After all, our justice system is based on the idea of repaying evil acts with punishment.

### 3. THE HEAVENLY LEVEL

Though the human level appeals to a sense of justice, it won't get us any closer to the level on which Jesus said we should live. That is the heavenly level where people return good for evil. Not many people live on this level consistently. It means doing good to people who try to hurt you, steal from you or cheat you.

It doesn't really make sense—unless you see it

from God's perspective. The Bible says that God is kind to the ungrateful and the wicked. (See Isaiah 26:10.) Is that because He likes ingratitude and wickedness? No. It's because His character doesn't change no matter how men behave. He is the source of all goodness, and the only way to counteract evil is with goodness.

> Do not be overcome by evil, but overcome evil with good.
> —ROMANS 12:21

## IF YOU HAVE GOD, YOU HAVE EVERYTHING.

The vast majority of people give to get. I believe we ought to give because we already have received. If you have God, you have everything.

The heavenly level is where we realize that God's supply of goodness has no end. We can afford to pour it out on friends and enemies alike without ever fearing that we'll run out. That's the level on which we're invited to live.

Let me restate the lessons I want you to draw from this chapter before we move on:

1. Giving is the only path to happiness.
2. As a Christian, you lack nothing.
3. There is no need to strive after God's promises.
4. Only giving will cause us to bear fruit.
5. You can give only what you have.

In the coming chapters we're going to break

down the components of the giving life and make a step-by-step plan to start giving ourselves away. But first I want to share with you my own journey of discovering this powerful principle.

# THREE

# HOW
# I GOT
# STARTED

Every great work has small beginnings. We give our little, and God gives a lot. Like anyone else, I wasn't born with the principle of giving fully developed in my life. It took years of trial and error, seeing how things worked, to "discover" it. I had to start by giving the little I had, and God responded by giving a lot in return.

One day I asked myself a simple question: How do I get God's attention? I knew if I could get His attention, I'd have His ear, His blessings and everything I needed.

So I looked in the Bible and found the answer, though it wasn't what I expected. The Bible gives us some examples of things that got God's attention:

- The fall of a common, ordinary sparrow (Matt. 10:29)
- A single strand of hair falling from someone's head (Matt. 10:30)

- The hungry cry of a tiny baby (Isa. 49:15)
- The sound of two small coins falling from a widow's hand (Mark 12:42)

These simple things got the attention of almighty God. As I read these verses, the pattern became clear. It isn't the high and mighty to whom God gives His attention—it's to the lowliest, neediest, poorest creatures of the earth.

When I made this discovery I determined to gather up the hurting people whom the world overlooked—the scroungy guy from downtown whom no one wanted to touch; the convalescent down to her last penny; the unwanted kids; the people who had failed and fallen. If I could reach out to them, I could get the attention of God.

IT ISN'T THE HIGH AND MIGHTY
TO WHOM GOD GIVES HIS
ATTENTION—IT'S TO THE
LOWLIEST, NEEDIEST, POOREST
CREATURES OF THE EARTH.

Reaching the hurting became the main plank of my ministry. Yes, I did it out of compassion, but I also did it because I knew that blessing follows when you reach down to people nobody else wants.

## CATCHING IT FROM DAD

I can't possibly overstate the influence my father had on me when it comes to giving. The old saying is true: *Some things are taught; some are caught.* I really caught my "giving-ness" from my dad. I never knew a more selfless man. He was totally devoted to reaching the lost and healing the hurting. He raised us in Armordale, a neighborhood in Kansas City that I now realize was a ghetto. It was an industrial area, and our house sat a hundred yards from the railroad tracks in a railroad yard.

My dad pastored a small church, but he used buses to pick people up for church on Sundays. I remember going door to door to tell people that the bus was coming on Sunday morning—and anyone who rode would get an ice cream bar.

Then there was my mother. Somehow, word got around in the hobo community that our house was generous with free meals. These train-riding bums would always show up at the door, and Mom would fix them something to eat while they waited outside on the steps. I can still picture her holding the plate of food in one hand, opening the door with the other and saying, "Step back from the door." When the hobo stepped back to give her room, she knew he would not make a move to rob the place. Then she set the plate on the step. He would eat it, sometimes thank her and then leave.

After observing this for a while, I asked why she fed all the hobos. She said, "Someday you may be away from home and need food, and I believe that by feeding others, I'm making sure that someone will feed you if you're ever in need."

I've been away from home most of my life

now, and I've always had a church willing to keep me fed. My mother's generosity worked!

People ridiculed my dad for giving himself to the poor. They thought he was trying to build a big church out of beggars and castoffs—and he was. He made no apology for that. He had holes in the bottoms of his shoes and wore the cheapest suits he could get because he wasn't thinking about himself—he was thinking about the people he was trying to reach.

I caught that spirit from him. Often I went with him to visit sick people in the hospital. I rode with him on Sunday morning bus routes. Doing these kinds of things with him became as important to me as any sermon—doing that was the gospel to me. As I studied the Bible and church history, I saw that every world-changing ministry started with ministry to the poor. Jesus certainly did. So did the Methodists and the early Pentecostals. History shows that every great denomination started among the poor and uneducated. Tragically, most denominations eventually grew bigger and more affluent and turned from the poor. When they made that turn, their spiritual vibrancy withered.

I was determined to focus my ministry on giving to the disenfranchised, the unwanted, the unwealthy. When I was thirteen I wanted to preach, but no church would have me. So I went to the mission downtown and preached to the drunks. They would get saved every time I came, but even that built faith in my heart. I grew to love them. I told myself that someday I would have a mission to help people like them.

I went to Davenport to pastor a church. Soon I started running buses as my dad had done. It wasn't long until we had forty-seven buses, more than in the city bus fleet. I admit that at first I had mixed motives. I knew you could generate excitement and momentum by doing something unusual. At that time no one was using buses to pick people up for church. That Davenport church needed a jump-start to jolt it out of its complacency, and buses were just the ticket.

> HE WASN'T THINKING ABOUT HIMSELF— HE WAS THINKING ABOUT THE PEOPLE HE WAS TRYING TO REACH.

But one day the bus brought a little girl who had broken her arm, and her parents hadn't bothered to set it. The bone was almost sticking out of her skin. When I saw that, my heart twisted inside of me, and a new compassion began to awaken. Other kids came with cigarette burns on their arms. My heart continued to change. My capacity for compassion deepened, and I became more like my dad in heart as well as in actions.

## DEEP IMPRESSIONS

There was another influence that pushed me to be a giver. It was the great healing revivals that were taking place when I was a boy. My father's church was very much a part of the early healing ministry. The first Voice of Healing convention was held at my dad's church. Jack Coe had the world's biggest tent pitched there. (As it turned out, a flood swept through the city and destroyed the tent and the church. It washed our ten buses down the river and took our home, robbing my family and me of our most precious possessions.)

William Branham and many other great men of faith have stayed at my dad's home. I remember Branham holding me on his lap one evening in our living room. I grew up on the front pew in those great crusades and witnessed that move of God up close. It was wonderful when it started. People were healed, signs and wonders were evident, and I believe God was trying to do something special.

But as the healing revival progressed, I saw it degenerate. Often I would see the same people going forward for healing at each crusade. I also saw evangelists tell people they were healed when they weren't.

The lead-in to the offering grew longer and more pressure-packed until I wondered, *If these men have such great faith, why do they need to take so much time asking for money?*

There were competitions over who had the biggest tent, the most impressive ministry, the biggest reputation or the most money pouring in. It seemed as though the revival had deteriorated from something pure to a tool to get glory and money.

I talked to my dad about it. I was planning on

entering the ministry, but I was troubled by what I had seen. My dad did something very wise; he asked me what I believed. I said I believed that Jesus saved and that we should reach the poor and hungry. That's what I'd grown up with, and I'd never seen that type of ministry abused. My dad nodded and told me to preach what I believed. That moment I made up my mind which way my ministry would go.

## "THESE SIGNS FOLLOW"

Of course I believe in healing. It needs to be a part of our ministry. But I don't believe in people being deceived. I have attended a lot of healing meetings where I left feeling as though I had been spiritually manipulated. The meetings were more about hype than healing.

> FEED PEOPLE, CLOTHE THEM AND WIN THEM TO CHRIST—AND THEN MIRACLES OF HEALING AND DELIVERANCE WILL HAPPEN BEFORE YOUR EYES.

Some men and women who make healing the focus of their ministries seem to presume that they can activate the gift of healing *at will.* I don't believe the gift of healing can be activated by the will of people. I believe the gift is activated by the will of the Holy Spirit, who "gives them to each one, just as he determines" (1 Cor. 12:11). Otherwise, we could walk into hospitals and empty them out.

On the other hand, when I have attended meetings where people were won to Christ, I have never left without feeling good and clean. And I have never felt spiritually manipulated in a feeding line. The Bible says, "These signs shall *follow* them that believe"—not *precede* them (Mark 16:17, KJV, emphasis added). Healing and other Spirit-activated gifts follow the one who wins the lost. While we're out helping people or preaching the gospel, we can lay hands on someone and that person will be healed.

So many preachers want the gifts to go before them to legitimize their ministry, but it doesn't work that way. Feed people, clothe them and win them to Christ—*and then* miracles of healing and deliverance will happen before your eyes.

I am a bona fide, blue-ribbon Pentecostal, born and raised in Holy Ghost fire, but what turns me on is leading people to Christ and healing the hurting. That's the hook to get them to Jesus. Winning souls is easy after you've given them clothes, a Thanksgiving turkey, bicycles, cleaned their streets, gotten rid of the graffiti on their homes and taught their children. They come to Christ because they've seen His character.

That's what giving is about.

## ABUSE OF THE GIFTS

When I was a young minister, Pentecostal churches seemed totally focused on the gifts of the Holy Spirit, especially the gift of prophecy. Christians came to church wanting to hear prophetic words, and the altar call for salvation began to fade in importance. There were a few years in the early part of my ministry when hardly any of the churches I visited gave calls for salvation. They wanted dramatic healings, prophetic words and manifestations of the Holy Spirit—some of which were completely out of order.

I became so discouraged by this that I wrote a letter to Jack Hyles, the great Baptist preacher and a hero of mine. I told him I was considering becoming a Baptist because so few people in Pentecostal circles were concerned with bringing people to Christ. "Do you believe in speaking in tongues?" he asked me in return.

I said yes.

"Then why don't you stay in your own denomination," he responded, "and build a great soulwinning church that will turn the tide within the denomination?"

That was a landmark moment for me. I decided that I would try to set a pattern of good works for others to follow. I would make soul-winning the number one focus of my ministry.

At the time I was an evangelist, and it wasn't always easy. Sometimes I would preach my heart out, pleading with people to come to Christ, only to have a prophetic utterance interrupt in the middle of the altar call and sidetrack what I felt God was trying to do. One time at the end of a service I gave a call for salvation, and twenty-five people stood to receive Christ. I was thrilled, but right in the middle of it someone else broke out with what they thought was a message in tongues. As it came forth, all twenty-five people sat down, and the altar call was destroyed. The people never came forward to accept Christ.

I totally believe that the gifts should operate in the church, but when operated properly they draw people *to* Christ, not drive them *away*. The Holy Spirit operates in beauty and order, drawing people to Christ.

I say all of this to clarify why I chose the kind of ministry I have. I wanted to build my ministry on giving—giving Christ to the lost, hope to the hopeless and food to the hungry. If I had chosen to build on prophecy or healing, I would have been untrue to myself, and my ministry would not have lasted. But because I did what was in my heart, I believe I have had a small part in helping the Pentecostal movement see the importance of soulwinning and outreach to the needy.

## BURDEN VS. CALL

I'm still learning this principle of giving. It's not easy to live a giving life. I heard a story about a missionary to Africa who worked hard before he ever got there to train for his assignment. He dreamed about it at night, studied at school, raised money, learned the language. He imagined that the people he was going to serve would be waiting for him with great anticipation. But he was disillusioned when he arrived in Africa and found Christ-rejecting men and women who had turned other missionaries away, killed some and were hardened against the gospel. He expected to be rewarded by God and men for making such a sacrifice. Instead, the ministry was hard, the people were suspicious and unkind, and the blessing of God seemed far away. After a year or two this missionary, feeling strongly entitled to an explanation from God, blew up. "Why would You send me to this thankless place?" he asked the Lord. "I don't care for these people. I have no love for them."

God spoke to that man and said, "If you don't do it out of a love for them, do it out of a love for Me. These are the people for whom My Son went to the cross."

From that day on, the missionary had the joy of the Lord in his work; he didn't need to hear the thanks of men. He knew he was doing something that pleased God, and that was enough.

DECIDE WHERE THE
REWARD COMES FROM.

Like that missionary, when I helped Matthew get the Dream Center up and running, I expected the neighborhoods around us to erupt with applause. I thought the poor and infirm, even the neighborhood gang members, would dance around us exclaiming, "You've come just in time to save us!"

Instead, people to whom we gave job training stole our computers. Gang members held guns to my son's head and threatened to take his life. Mothers took our food without saying thanks. I asked God why we were there if they were so ungrateful.

He reminded me that we were there *for Him*, not for us. He loved them, and He didn't need the outward signs to know that changes were happening in hearts.

I learned a couple of lessons from those early years. First, decide where the reward comes from. If it comes from men, you'll always be frustrated. If it comes from God, you will always be satisfied.

Doing right has a built-in reward. You shouldn't need someone to brag on you. Having learned that, I can take joy from even the bleakest circumstances. Many times after helping someone late at night when others were asleep and my body ached to be in bed, I've walked away rejoicing, and I thought, *Wow! I got to help somebody.*

I had developed an appetite for the true reward.

Some pastors leave the ministry because they say that no one appreciates them. The problem is in their own hearts. If God appreciates you, that is reward enough.

God confirmed another issue for me in the start-up years at the Dream Center. It's important to have a *call*, not just a burden. Many people come to the Dream Center—youth groups, women's groups, men's groups—all sorts of teams from across America. I have learned that once people are in that inner-city environment, witnessing the poverty and sadness up close, it's easy to feel a burden for that kind of ministry.

But a burden is different from a call. If everyone who visited the Dream Center and felt a burden for the inner city decided to devote their lives to it, then thousands of people would flood into Los Angeles. And most of them, after a few months or a year, would become discouraged and go home.

Why? Because they followed a burden to Los Angeles—not a call.

GIVING IS A DECISION OF
THE WILL, NOT OF THE EMOTIONS.

You should never go into a ministry just because you have a burden for it. Burdens come and go. They are like feelings. I felt a burden for nearly every city I visited as a young man—from Calcutta, India to New York City. But I couldn't possibly devote my life to each one.

A *call* is different. It's a commitment that remains no matter what feelings come and go. It's a heart knowledge that you belong somewhere. It doesn't fade away as burdens do.

This morning when I woke up and caught an early plane from Phoenix to Los Angeles, I felt no burden for the poor in LA. I don't remember feeling much of anything, least of all compassion. What kept me going? *The call.*

The call gets you up in the morning, keeps you going when people criticize or misjudge you or when you run out of money. The call is hard to shake. It points like an inner compass to the place you know you ought to go. It may even contradict your emotions at times, but it's consistent.

That's how giving is, too. Giving is a decision of the will, not of the emotions.

What I've given you in this chapter is just an overview—a sketch—of how I began to learn about the principle of giving. I know I still have a long way to go. We all do. To help us grow, in the following chapters I want to apply this principle of giving to seven specific areas of our lives. By the time we finish, I think you'll agree that the results are life changing.

# FOUR

# THE MOST IMPORTANT THING YOU OWN

Some time ago I was on a trip to preach in another city. After the Sunday morning service the pastor told me a man was there who had expressed a strong desire to see me. This man wanted to drive me back to my hotel so he could talk with me. He had already driven one hundred miles for the opportunity.

I hesitated. I was tired from preaching and wanted to relax. I had learned that once people start talking, often they don't want to stop. I didn't want him to cut into my afternoon time, which I use to pray and stay focused on the message for the evening service. The pastor assured me that the man only wanted to drive me to the hotel. That would be enough. Sighing, I agreed. The man pulled his car around to pick me up.

To my surprise he was a pleasant, levelheaded person. As he drove, we chatted about various things. But I kept waiting for him to come to his real purpose. After all, if he'd driven such a distance, he must have a problem or an idea or something to talk about. Usually, when a man insists upon seeing me, he wants to talk about his wife leaving him or about a financial problem or advice about how to pursue God's call on his life. This man didn't bring anything up, and we kept conversing about everyday things.

We arrived at the hotel, and he pulled up to the front door. He put the car in park and smiled at me. I was anxious to broach the subject, so I asked how I could help him. "Is there some advice you were seeking, or do you have a problem that you wanted to discuss?" I asked.

His answer took me by surprise. "No," he said with no sense of urgency. "There's nothing specific. I just love you, Pastor Barnett, and wanted to be with you."

I was bewildered and grateful all at once! I shook his hand, and we parted ways, never to see each other again. As I walked to my room I marveled that this man had driven so far to spend just fifteen minutes with me. He had discovered something few people discover—the value of time and togetherness.

## A PRICELESS COMMODITY

*Time* is the single most valuable thing any of us own. Although God's resources of peace, joy, money and hope are unlimited, time is not. In fact, God cannot give time away as humans can. He is timeless and eternal. If He gives you one minute of His time, His supply of time is not reduced one bit. He'll never die.

Not so for us. When we give time, it costs us life itself. God has placed a limit on how long we live—one hundred twenty years at the most, and usually only into our mid-seventies. The length of your life is determined by so many things—from eating habits to your DNA—but none of us can make life go on forever.

### TIME IS THE SINGLE MOST VALUABLE THING ANY OF US OWN.

Life is something we are constantly losing. The apostle Paul said, "Outwardly we are wasting away..." (2 Cor. 4:16). As we sit, work, sleep and play, we're moving closer toward death, one minute at a time. That's why I take every meeting, every conversation, every moment seriously—because it's costing me and other people the most important thing we own.

When I preach, I am keenly aware that every person listening is moving toward death one moment at a time. The time they give to hearing what I say is more valuable than anything any of us own.

When people tell me they have nothing to give, I ask, "Do you have time?" Everyone has it. For many years I have preached a sermon titled "There's a Miracle in Your House." It's about giving what you have and letting God miraculously provide the rest, just as the widow did in Elisha's day as she poured the endless supply of oil into her jars and saved herself and her sons from being sold into slavery. (See 2 Kings 4:1–7.)

Time is something we all have. It's the stuff of miracles. We don't need any prior success to start putting our time to use. Time may be the only thing you have—then use it!

The man who drove me to the hotel treated time as a valuable commodity, and he apportioned it wisely. The best way to use the precious resource of time is by giving it away deliberately and wisely. We must realize that when we invest time in God and in people, we get every second of it back in more ways than we can imagine.

## THE HOMEBODY

People think that I must be so busy that I don't really have a family life. They imagine me flying every day to preach here and there, always holding conferences, bouncing back and forth between my churches in Phoenix and Los Angeles.

THE BEST WAY TO USE
THE PRECIOUS RESOURCE
OF TIME IS BY GIVING IT
AWAY DELIBERATELY AND WISELY.

In truth, I'm much more of a homebody than most people realize. From the day I got married and started having children, I put them at the head of my schedule. I refused to let church activities dominate my time. I only went to church on church nights. People would invite me to dinners and potluck suppers and other fun activities, but I told them I had a previous appointment. I even stood in the pulpit one time and told my flock this: "I can either be your buddy—eating dinner with you and playing golf all the time—or I can be a man of God and keep my family together."

I discovered that when I gave time to my family, God gave me both a great church and a great family. I spent my kids' childhood years going to football and basketball games, wrestling matches and school programs. I limited my midweek travel so it wouldn't put a strain on my wife. At the time I don't think I realized how great the benefits would be later on. I now have the family I've always dreamed of having. My sons and daughter have grown up to honor God, and they give so much back to me without even knowing it. Without question, my kids are the single biggest blessing God has given me.

I recognized how great the return was one night after church. I had stayed after the Sunday night service to counsel someone, and it was a long counseling session. When I came out I expected everyone else to be gone, but sitting on the curb was Matthew, a teenager at the time. He looked up at me and smiled. "Matthew," I asked, "why are you still here? I thought you'd be out with your friends." He stood up, and we began walking to the car.

"Well, Dad," he said, "I got to thinking about all the people in the world who want to spend time with you, and all the pastors who say nice things about you. I decided that of all the things I could be doing, I want to spend time with you.

I've been out here waiting and looking forward to driving home with you."

We got in the car, but it was hard to drive with those tears in my eyes!

You can't predict the kinds of wonderful pay-offs that come when you invest time in your children. Every Monday I get a call from my son Luke while I'm reading the paper and drinking my Starbucks coffee. He shares with me all the things that happened during the Sunday before. He tells about the altar calls, the offerings, the victories, the things little and big that make pastoring a joy. And when he's had a rough day he cries on my shoulder.

A little later, usually around noon, Matthew calls me and does the same thing, sharing about the day before. I used to do the same thing and call my dad every Monday to share the victories and experiences of the day before. Now I get all the payback for the time I invested in Luke and Matthew when they were just children. They come back to me voluntarily, and nothing makes me feel more honored or loved.

## TOGETHERNESS WITH GOD

It is also just as important to give time to God.

Behind all the big events and fun we have at Phoenix First Assembly is a church that prays, one that runs to the Father for answers. That's why things work. People think we're fueled by good ideas, money or enthusiasm, but it's really our investment of time in prayer that makes Phoenix First a world-class church.

Some people spend time with God in the same way they spend time in the hospital—only when necessary and as briefly as possible. But the Bible says, "In *all* your ways acknowledge him"—not just in problem times (Prov. 3:6).

> YOU CAN BUY INFLUENCE
> AND KNOWLEDGE AND
> ALL SORTS OF OTHER THINGS,
> BUT YOU CAN'T BUY CHARACTER.

We should run to Him at all times. I am more aware of my dependence on God now than when I started in the ministry. I used to have devotional times; now I have a devotional life. I used to pray in the mornings; now I pray all day. I want to give God every minute I have—not an hour here or there.

I must admit that I haven't gotten *stronger* with maturity; I've gotten *weaker*. I don't know nearly as much as I thought I did when I was a young man. In times with God I've learned to fear my strength, and that has pushed me to spend even more time with God—all the time I can, so that His character is impressed on the clay of my life. That's the only way to change. Education won't do it. You can buy influence and knowledge and all sorts of other things, but you can't buy character. That only comes through spending time with God.

There are some things we can only get when we give time to God. For example, my wife can tell me some things when we are in public, but other things are only appropriate to talk about at the table when the company is gone but the kids are with us. And some things she can only say when we're alone. There are levels of intimacy that must be developed.

It's the same way with God. When we invest that alone time with Him, He speaks to us in ways He can't speak to us when we're with other people.

## DRIVEN TO TIME WITH GOD

When we don't give time to God, in His love He may force us into situations where we must spend time with Him. Some of us are afraid of being face to face, eyeball to eyeball with God. We don't know what He'll say to us. We feel that if we're with Him for too long, He might summon us to an impossible level of service or humiliate us with our sins.

After a service one time, I met a lady who said she didn't want to be close to God. She just wanted to be close enough to get to heaven. She told me that in high school she purposely earned Cs because making As would have meant people expected more of her, and making Fs would have meant failure. She conducted her spiritual life in much the same way.

What an awful way to live! She withheld time from God for worthless reasons.

One of the hardest times of my life was when my father died. I was left without someone with whom I could laugh and cry. I was driven to solitude with God as a source of strength, and I found an intimacy with Him I had never known.

Another very difficult time—perhaps the darkest time in my life—was in the late 1980s when Jimmy Swaggart and Jim Bakker fell because of moral failures. As the pastor of the largest Assembly of God church in the United States, I received calls from *Nightline, Crossfire* and other shows asking that I appear on their programs. But I felt God speak to my heart and tell me to go hide myself and learn who He was.

As difficult as those days and months were, and as much as it felt as if the church at large was caving in around me, I made more spiritual advancement during that time than any other. I learned that the Holy Spirit is a person. I learned what God is like and about His mercy and His love.

God uses difficult circumstances to teach us. Whether or not you spend time alone with God in the good times, I can promise you that someday you will be forced into time with Him in bad times. I think of Elijah who was summoned to the brook Kerith to spend time being fed by ravens and drinking from the stream there. (See 1 Kings 17.) Those were good times for Elijah. But later he ran into the desert, burned out and wanting to die.

But in the desert, in the midst of his difficult circumstances, he learned more about who God is.

God took Israel to the desert so they might be alone with Him and so that He could teach them. He forced time together, and He'll do the same for us. That's how much He loves us.

## BEING THERE

The trials I've gone through have taught me how to invest time with God. Even if He doesn't give me a new idea or a specific answer to whatever concern I have, there is a heart exchange that is invaluable to me. Just being with Him is enough.

For years I went to a ledge on the mountain behind my church and prayed at the same time every day. One day I arrived to see a young man on the ledge above me. We waved to each other, but we didn't speak a word.

He was there the next day and every day after that for weeks. We never spoke, only waved; sometimes we didn't acknowledge each other at all.

One day I found a letter on my windshield. It was from him, and it read, "I know you wonder why I go to the ledge above you. I haven't wanted to bother you because I know that time of prayer is special to you. I've been going through a crisis and needed that time alone. I felt that if I could get close to you, it would help me face the crisis. You don't know how it's helped me."

He never asked for counsel or advice. He was just there. We were in each other's presence.

That's how it can be with God.

When I was a boy I idolized my father and watched everything he did. I sat in his office when he counseled people. I watched him study the Word, take naps in the darkened sanctuary, walk and pray at the altar. I admired everything about him, even the way he would drive with his arm out the window. I decided that one day I would do everything just as he did.

That's how it is with God. It's not always about talking. It's about being together. Some preachers see the devil everywhere, and they live in the constant awareness of Satan. I try to live in the constant awareness of God who permeates the atmosphere in which we live. We can choose whose presence we are more aware of, and I choose God every time.

Sometimes you come to Him with nothing to say. You're not happy enough to shout, not sad enough to cry, and you're not going to complain. You just want to hang out with Him.

> IT'S NOT ALWAYS
> ABOUT TALKING. IT'S
> ABOUT BEING TOGETHER.

It reminds me of these old-timers I see around Phoenix who sit around whittling and spitting but not saying anything. They just want to be in each other's presence.

A group of researchers recently did an analysis of our church. They asked me what my favorite hobby was. At one time I would have said golf. But in all sincerity, this time I said, "Quiet moments with God." That's when I hear His voice.

## BORN IN PRAYER

The return on your investment of time with

God and people will be larger than you can imagine. As I learn the sacred value of time and balance the use of my time, I find God shoring me up in ways I couldn't predict. For example, when I was firm about giving the better part of my free time to my family, I found that God brought me highly qualified, highly effective and innovative staff members to help fulfill our church's vision. With them, our church accomplished vastly more than if I had sweated and labored to do everything myself.

I also found that God helped us to work efficiently. Less time was wasted staring at the walls or waiting on other people because we knew time was valuable. When it was time to work, we worked. When it was time to relax, we relaxed. And God seemed to grant us favor by speeding things up for us.

Many people know of the pastor's schools we hold in Phoenix and Los Angeles. This year the attendance will be around fourteen thousand. But most people don't know that the idea for the pastor's schools did not come from some brilliant strategy session—it was birthed out of a desire to make the best use of our time as a pastoral staff.

I was in Davenport at the time. As we began to grow, more and more people came by to learn how to make their churches grow, too. My time, and my staff members' time, was being taken up with people wanting advice. So we made a practical decision and set aside a day to share all the knowledge we had about church growth. That was the first pastor's school, and the response was so good that we did it again the next year, extending it to two days. Now we've done it for twenty-five years, and it's the largest pastor's school in the world.

But it started with the desire to use time wisely, to give time away.

Every good idea I've had for ministry came during prayer times. Our Master's Commission was born during an intensive time of prayer and Bible study with Larry Kerychuck and a new convert. I would guess that nearly every other ministry in our church was born in times of prayer as well.

When, as an evangelist, I held a meeting in Hutchison, Kansas, I met a man named Henry Krauss who was developing a new type of plow. One day he hit a snag, and he couldn't figure out how to make a particular part of the plow work. He was stumped by this one little problem. He became so wrapped up in fixing it that he thought, *I'll skip the prayer meeting tonight and work on this problem.* But he thought better of it. *No, I'd better be faithful.* So off to Wednesday night prayer he went. That night while he was on his knees at the altar, God gave him the idea he needed. As a result, he was able to complete the Krauss plow, which was a huge success and enabled him to give millions to the work of God.

## THE HALF-HOUR

One day God gave me an idea that revolutionized how I used time. I call it *The Lesson of the Half-Hours.*

I was studying Revelation 8 and came across this passage:

> When he opened the seventh seal, there was silence in heaven for about half an hour.
> —REVELATION 8:1

This is the only place in the Bible where heaven is measured in time—these strange few moments when silence takes over before yielding to an eternal chorus of worship. Elsewhere Jesus says He is the "I AM," meaning He is beyond time (Exod. 3:14). But here, for just a moment, eternity is measured.

TELL ME WHAT YOU DO WITH YOUR HALF-HOURS, AND I'LL TELL YOU WHAT YOUR LIFE IS.

That told me that if it was important enough to God to mention this thirty-minute segment of eternity, then it must be important for us. He could have said a *year* or a *month*, but it was only thirty minutes. Suddenly I began seeing life through new eyes—and I realized that half-hours are important to God.

Tell me what you do with your half-hours, and I'll tell you what your life is. Leave alone what you want to do in the next year or six months—it's the half-hours that count. The half-hour right after you get up in the morning. The half-hour spent waiting for your meal to arrive at the restaurant or waiting for the bus or waiting to go to bed.

No great work is built in years or decades. Everything that's worthwhile has been done in half-hours. As the old poem says:

> Little drops of water,
> Little grains of sand,
> Make the mighty ocean
> And the pleasant land.[1]

It's what you do with your little things that add up to something big. Pennies make dollars. Minutes make lifetimes. And half-hours determine your future.

Think of what happens in half-hours:

- You can be married in less than a half-hour.
- You can make a life-changing decision in half an hour.
- Most people accept Christ in the space of a half-hour.
- Most are called into the ministry in half an hour.

You are as good a Christian as are your half-hours.

When I looked at my life as a series of half-hours, I began to find a lot of empty space. Space at the airport waiting to board an airplane or on the plane waiting to land. Space at my hotel room after an evening service or sitting in the pastor's office waiting for him to return.

I decided to start using those half-hours! I began to bring magazines and books with me on every trip, and I enriched my mind and soul with them, using time that otherwise would have been wasted.

When I went somewhere to preach and the pastor left me in his office, I started going through his books, reading here and there, learning.

I started using "down time" to prepare my sermons. A sermon usually takes four to six hours to prepare, but most of my sermon preparation is done in half-hour segments.

Every book I've written was completed in half-hours.

Most counseling is done in half-hours.

One time the Barnetts were traveling as a family to Ohio for Thanksgiving, and we sat in facing rows of seats on a Southwest Airlines plane. Around this time Matthew was writing his book *The Church That Never Sleeps.* We were all joking around as a family, enjoying the time together, when Matthew quietly pulled out his computer and began tapping. We hardly noticed that he had left the conversation, but a little while later I saw him put the computer away. I asked what he'd done. "Wrote another chapter for the book," he said.

That's called using your half-hours!

I often hear people say, "I want to serve God my whole life."

I say, "Why not serve Him half an hour a day to start?" You can clean up a lot of streets in thirty minutes. You can adopt your block. You can win a soul. You can do anything you want with thirty minutes.

- The difference between an A or a B is half an hour a day.

- The difference between a clean and a dirty house...
- Between wealth and a midlevel income...
- A half-hour could make the difference in how your kids turn out.

On the other hand, lives are ruined in half-hour segments. A brief escapade, an error in judgment, a lapse of morals can steal countless fruitful hours from an otherwise bright future.

"WHY NOT SERVE HIM
HALF AN HOUR A DAY TO START?"

I often meet with ministers who need some sort of advice—usually for the space of a half-hour. During those half-hours, entire ministries have been saved.

When we see each half-hour we have as important, we have traveled a long way toward making our time count.

In this chapter we have talked about several ways to give our time:

1. Give time to your family.
2. Give time to God.
3. Give time to other people.

Discovering the joy—and the benefits—of giving your time will yield a great harvest in your life. When you have successfully discovered the hidden power of giving away yourself through your time, God will:

1. Make your time more effective.

2. Surround you with people to do the work with you.

3. Help you find time that otherwise would have been lost.

4. Bless you richly in your family relationships.

5. Give you spiritual depth that comes from being with Him.

In the next chapter we'll talk about giving away something less valuable but often more coveted than time.

# FIVE

# GIVING
# MONEY

The *Los Angeles Times* called it the largest Christmas giveaway in history.

For Christmas 2000, our people at the Dream Center wanted to do something great. They brainstormed and came up with an idea to adopt five hundred city blocks surrounding the Center and to provide food and gifts for every household. Our normal Adopt-a-Block ministry reaches eighty-five blocks. I like big plans, but I said, "Do you know what you're up against? Do some research, and tell me if you really mean it."

The staff discovered that five hundred blocks meant forty-five thousand homes and two hundred fifty thousand people. This five-hundred-block area is the size of Des Moines, Iowa or Colorado Springs. Still, the staff thought they could do it, and I said, "Praise God." But I didn't really think they could pull it off.

They started calling around, getting donations. They rounded up three million dollars' worth of gifts in kind. It took days to wrap two hundred fifty thousand presents and three warehouses to store the food and gifts. But as the season wore on, it looked as if they might be successful. They adopted the blocks from Skid Row past Dodger Stadium to Hollywood and South Central.

The night before the giveaway, we rented trucks, packed them full and sent them to the neighborhoods to deliver large pallets of gifts. Guards stayed all night to guard the trucks. That next morning, seven thousand volunteers turned out to distribute presents. We rented buses to take the volunteers to their assigned blocks, and in six hours we had visited everyone in that five-hundred-block area. More than six thousand people signed decision cards that day.

GOD DOESN'T ASK US TO
GIVE ONLY WHAT WE CAN
AFFORD—HE ASKS US TO
GIVE WHAT WE CAN'T AFFORD.

It was one of the most amazing days of my life—and in the history of Los Angeles. Never before had so many people received so much help in such a short period of time. Never before had that many volunteers been mobilized.

That one day cost us $400,000, and it took months to pay off the debt. But that's what we're about—giving money and winning souls.

## REASON FOR SUCCESS

The reason the Dream Center has grown so rapidly and become such a hub for ministry is that we are constantly giving. That's the purpose for its existence. Every day we give away thousands of dollars worth of clothes, food, education, medicine and job training. We clean the streets, mow people's lawns, provide transportation and conduct sidewalk Sunday school. And we ask ourselves, "What can we give away next?"

The Dream Center costs hundreds of thousands of dollars every month to operate. Essentially we give away millions of dollars a year to our surrounding community. But as we do, the most marvelous thing happens: God brings that money full circle and replenishes our reserves so we can keep on giving!

I am absolutely convinced that the only way to keep money flowing through your hands is to give it away. Yet many Christians live with fists clenched. Have you ever noticed that some Christians say they believe God provides for their material needs, but they continue to live as if God keeps them on a limited stipend? They plan small, live small and keep their vision small because they can't fathom that God might want to send more money through them. A little money flows in—just enough to pay the bills— and a little money flows out as they give only what they think they can afford.

But God doesn't ask us to give only what we can afford—He asks us to give what we can't afford. He asks us to give as if our supply were unlimited.

I have watched it happen over and over in my ministry and in other people's ministries. When a man is stingy with God, God is stingy with him. When a ministry keeps money to itself, it dies. But when a ministry gives beyond what it has, the storehouses of heaven open wide.

Am I saying money grows on trees? No, it's better than that. Money grows *in God's hands*, and He gives it to people who give it away.

MONEY IS NOT GOOD
OR EVIL IN ITSELF. IT IS LIKE A
MIRROR, REFLECTING THE HEART
AND CHARACTER OF ITS OWNER.

Money is God's way of testing our mettle. It's a touchstone that shows us what we're made of on the inside. A stingy person shows lack of faith. A greedy person shows selfishness. A profligate person shows lack of discipline. That's why Jesus told so many parables about money—because few things so readily reveal a man's heart.

Money can do a lot of things—influence politics, drive the world economy, determine the fate of nations—but the single most important thing about money is not what it does, but our attitude toward it. Money is not good or evil in itself. It is like a mirror, reflecting the heart and character of its owner. Of course, the kingdom is not meat or drink or money, but there is a very real relationship between the kingdom and money. Luke tells us this:

> So if you have not been trustworthy in han-
> dling worldly wealth, who will trust you with
> true riches?
>
> —LUKE 16:11

So how do we give money away? What are the "secrets" that make this principle work? Let's take a look.

## SAVING UP

I have discovered this: God wants us to be givers, just as He is. The more we give or sow or invest, the more God will entrust to us. The only way to turn the spigot on and increase the amount of money God entrusts to us is to give away what we already have.

Let me give you an example. When I was a teenage evangelist preaching around the world, I decided to start saving up money. I didn't have a lot to save. In those days, churches would invite a guest preacher or evangelist like myself for a week of ministry, give him a small food budget and take one love offering to cover his entire stay. That means I would work for five to seven days, and they would pay me with whatever came in during a single offering, plus the food budget.

It was hard to live on that!

By contrast, churches today take love offerings sometimes in every service for a visiting evange-list. And if it doesn't meet a certain minimum, the church ups the amount to something accept-able. They also put you up in hotels, whereas I spent a good portion of my early traveling years sleeping in the pastor's extra bedroom or church apartment.

Nevertheless, I started to plan and save. I ate "on the cheap" and saved the food budget. I stashed away as much of what I earned as I could. After a few years I had a whopping $8,700, which I put in a mutual fund. My dad told me never to touch it because it was my retirement money. Being a minister, I had opted out of social security.

> GOD WANTS US TO
> BE GIVERS, JUST AS HE
> IS. THE MORE WE GIVE OR
> SOW OR INVEST, THE MORE
> GOD WILL ENTRUST TO US.

I didn't add anything to it, but by the time I went to Phoenix twenty years later, it had grown to almost $200,000. Compound interest had kicked in, and my teenage planning had earned me the beginnings of a retirement nest egg.

That money gave me a great sense of safety and security. I felt I had something to fall back on. It also fueled my dreams of traveling, buying a house and providing for my family. I had planned wisely and was happy to have taken away the worry of retirement.

## THE CHALLENGE TO GIVE

Soon after I arrived in Phoenix the church embarked on an ambitious plan to build one of the biggest churches in America at that time. It would seat seven thousand people, have three levels and two balconies on the inside and be set against a beautiful mountain overlooking Phoenix. It would cost several million dollars, an astounding amount of money in those days for a medium-sized inner-city church like us.

As a congregation we started casting and recasting the vision, making sure everyone understood it. We wanted all the people to be excited about what the Lord would do once we had built the new place. One Sunday morning I had everyone bring the largest gift they had ever given and place it in what we called our *Joash chest*, a chest like the one they had in the Bible when they renovated the temple.

That day was one of the most spiritually charged days of my life. There was a Holy Spirit electricity coursing through the auditorium as I watched people bring deeds to homes, titles for cars, rings, gold, silver and insurance policies and put them into the Joash chest. The raw materials for carrying out the vision were assembling before me, and I was grateful and humbled. I had never seen people respond like that before.

I too had brought a several-thousand-dollar gift to put in the chest, but as the parade of giving continued and I watched people make real sacrifices, the Lord spoke the unthinkable to me: "Give your mutual fund."

If I hadn't known better, I would have thought my mind was playing tricks on me, caught up in the emotion of the moment. But I knew better. I had not heard the words audibly, but the conviction was strong in my heart.

I called my family up to the platform—my wife, two sons and daughter—and in private told them what I felt was the right thing to do. But I was leaving the decision up to them. I wouldn't give the fund if they didn't agree because this was their inheritance. If they had disagreed or demurred in any way, I would not have given it. That's how strongly I felt about guarding this significant portion of money we had saved.

My boys, young as they were, were quick to say, "Give it, Dad!"

Then my daughter, face filled with concern, asked if it meant she would never have a new dress. Holding back the tears, I assured her it didn't mean that at all.

My wife, who knew what this meant to us, asked if God had told me to do it. This was the only money we had saved aside from $17,000 that I had received from the sale of our house in Davenport, Iowa when we moved to Arizona. I didn't want to manipulate her emotions or twist her arm in any way, so I said I didn't know if God had told me—not fully, anyway. I only had a strong conviction. I was not willing to pull the trump card out of my sleeve by insisting, "Thus saith the Lord." We were free to make the decision together under the guidance of the Holy Spirit.

She looked at me for a moment, then said if I felt it was the right thing to do, we should give it. So that day, against all worldly wisdom—and even my dad's best advice—we joined the parade of sacrifice, took all the money in the mutual fund and laid it in the Joash chest. I felt a burst of freedom at having given something that meant so much to me. I was back in God's hands again.

The new church was built and dedicated, and it became the site of countless conferences, services, meetings and moments of inspiration. And I got used to living without that nest egg.

But not long after that I took that money we had made from the sale of our house in Iowa and bought ten acres in the desert near Phoenix. All my friends in real estate told me it was a bad buy, but I had a hunch. I put $17,000 down on a $60,000 parcel, and then went about the business of my life, making the payments, checking in on my investment every now and then.

A few years later a developer decided that part of the desert was the perfect place to put in a Jack Nicklaus golf course. When he did, it drove the value of my parcel up to $375,000. The Lord had restored our $200,000 retirement—plus 80 percent!

Later as we prepared to build a Sunday school complex, God spoke to me again. This time He told me to give the $375,000 property to the church to start the building program. The gift would be a seed to inspire others. God used this sacrifice to jump-start the project!

## THE HEART OF A GIVER

I've seen that kind of return over and over again as I have given money to God's work, and I have

learned that investing pleases God. It might
seem to make sense that hoarding is the only way
to accumulate wealth. But remember that the
kingdom works backwards. In God's economy,
you gain what you lose and lose what you gain.
The only way to keep money is to give it away.

We are the only ones who can limit what God
wants to give through us. He wants to be a
gusher in our lives, but many of us stop at a
trickle. The prodigal son's father said, "You are
always with me, and everything I have is yours"
(Luke 15:31). That tells me that, as a member of
God's household, God will take care of me in
every way. I can give liberally because my Father
is wealthy.

## IN GOD'S ECONOMY, YOU GAIN WHAT YOU LOSE AND LOSE WHAT YOU GAIN.

God wants to give Christian men and women
wealth so they can use it rightly. David Yonggi
Cho, the pastor of the world's largest church in
Seoul, South Korea, one time brought a group of
one hundred millionaires with him to a Christian
university in America where they were considering sending their children to school. Cho said
he had ten thousand other millionaires in his
congregation, and each one believed his purpose
in life was to make wealth to propagate the gospel
around the world. These people realized that
money has redemptive qualities and that entre-
preneurs are key players in kingdom work.

Of course, that's not the American dream. Most people go about life spending on their own desires and finding increasingly strange ways to pamper themselves. Some wealthy people are starting to invest large amounts of money in family tombs. Ruth Fertel, the founder of Ruth's Chris Steakhouse, recently built a twenty-seven-foot mausoleum on the edge of a bayou in her home state of Louisiana, and invited one hundred fifty friends and family to have hors d'oeuvres and celebrate its completion! The elaborate burial plot cost around half a million dollars.[1]

Another restaurant founder, Al Copeland of Popeye's Fried Chicken, commissioned a family tomb that will hold fourteen caskets for a cost of about $600,000![2]

It's OK to want a nice funeral, but think of what could be done, ministry-wise, with half a million dollars! Think how God would have been blessed them had they given that money away.

In Matthew 25, Jesus told the familiar story of the wise and foolish investors. These verses hold key principles about how to give our money away:

> Again, it [the kingdom of heaven] will be like a man going on a journey, who called his servants and entrusted his property to them. To one he gave five talents of money, to another two talents, and to another one talent, each according to his ability. Then he went on his journey. The man who had received the five talents went at once and put his money to work and gained

five more. So also, the one with the two talents gained two more. But the man who had received the one talent went off, dug a hole in the ground and hid his master's money.

After a long time the master of those servants returned and settled accounts with them. The man who had received the five talents brought the other five. "Master," he said, "you entrusted me with five talents. See, I have gained five more."

His master replied, "Well done, good and faithful servant! You have been faithful with a few things; I will put you in charge of many things. Come and share your master's happiness!"

The man with the two talents also came. "Master," he said, "you entrusted me with two talents; see, I have gained two more."

His master replied, "Well done, good and faithful servant! You have been faithful with a few things; I will put you in charge of many things. Come and share your master's happiness!"

Then the man who had received the one talent came. "Master," he said, "I knew that you are a hard man, harvesting where you have not sown and gathering where you have not scattered seed. So I was afraid and went out and hid your talent in the ground. See, here is what belongs to you."

His master replied, "You wicked, lazy servant! So you knew that I harvest where I have not sown and gather where I have not scattered seed? Well then, you should have put my money on deposit with the bankers, so that when I returned I would have received it back with interest.

"Take the talent from him and give it to the one who has the ten talents. For everyone who

> has will be given more, and he will have an abundance. Whoever does not have, even what he has will be taken from him. And throw that worthless servant outside, into the darkness, where there will be weeping and gnashing of teeth."
>
> —MATTHEW 25:14–30

There are ten things we can learn from this passage.

## 1. GOD GIVES MONEY TO PEOPLE.

Sometimes I wonder why God has any faith in people at all. He could have invested the money Himself or sent angels with heavenly bank accounts to keep a tight rein on the budget, but He didn't. He gave money to people.

We too must learn to give money to people. It sounds simple, but how many times have you wished you could bypass people altogether and simply write God a check? Or toss the money into the air for Him to catch?

There's an innate distrust of people, which keeps us from being generous. But if we are to be givers, we have no choice. We have to follow His example, take a deep breath and plunge in.

After all, God put the awesome responsibility of the kingdom in the hands of failing men—the disciples. These same men had denied and cursed Him. And He put His Spirit in people like you and me, as imperfect as we are. Then Jesus went to heaven and left us to run things under the Holy Spirit's guidance!

I can't say it's the way I would do things, but it was His choice, and so it's the best way. Get used to giving money to people. It's all we have.

## 2. THE LORD CHOOSES THE PEOPLE IN WHOM HE INVESTS.

Yes, we have to invest in people, but we have a choice of whom to invest in! This story tells us that God invests in all sorts of different people, from the faithful to the unfaithful. He gives everyone a chance, like the farmer scattering seed all over the ground. Some of it yields good fruit; some doesn't.

On the other hand, no master or investor is going to invest in obviously poor soil. No farmer throws seeds into bramble bushes, and no master seeks out lazy men. We have a choice in whom we will invest, but it should be balanced by a desire to give all men a chance to prove themselves wise, as God did with the servants in the story.

## 3. THE LORD IS WILLING TO RELEASE CONTROL TO THE PEOPLE IN WHOM HE INVESTS.

In the story, the master went away for a long time. He didn't send messengers to check on his investment, and he didn't micromanage the money he'd left behind. He simply let the servants do what they wished.

When you invest, you must lose control of that money. It's hard, but it's the only way. If you give money and then spend your time trying to make sure every cent of it is accounted for, you'll drive yourself crazy. Giving is supposed to liberate us, not keep us bound up in knots.

When we give money, we must also give trust.

### 4. THE LORD IS WILLING TO RISK.

When you give money to a charity, you want to see results. Even if you give to a bum on the street, you're hoping it produces something good. You don't want your money (which represents your time and hard work) going to waste.

> WHEN WE GIVE MONEY,
> WE MUST ALSO GIVE TRUST.

And yet the name of the game is *risk*. God is more like a venture capitalist than a miserly bank accountant. He plays a high-risk, high-reward game when He invests in us.

Christians sorely underestimate God as an investor. We are much more risk-averse than He is. It's as if someone painted a portrait of a heavenly Scrooge in the sky and convinced us that God is tightfisted. We tend to see Him in natural terms rather than supernatural ones.

- But God is not a miser.
- He is not worried about risking too much.
- He is not fearful of having too little.
- He is not worried that you will give away too much.

Remember that the kingdom works backward from what we expect.

God took a huge risk by investing His Spirit in you and me, and yet He is still reaping returns. Jesus is the most profitable investor in all of history, because He took one life, His own, and turned it into billions of lives when He died on the cross. He now lives many times over through other people. It's not magic—it's investment. As the Bible says, "Unless a kernel of wheat falls to the ground and dies, it remains only a single seed" (John 12:24).

God is willing to do the same with money. If He can take a chance on us, shouldn't we take a chance on someone else? And shouldn't we be merciful when that risk doesn't pay off?

An investment is not a guarantee. I never take money from someone who doesn't understand that it's a risk. It's wheat in the ground, and not all grains grow up. But if you sow enough, you'll still get a good harvest.

I know that not all the ministries in my church will go the distance. Not all people that come to my altar will finish strong. I'm not heartbroken when I don't get 100 percent return. I try to remind myself that Jesus took a risk, and I should, too.

## 5. RESOURCES ARE FOR USE, NOT FOR HOARDING.

God is not a miser but a distributor, an investor. He said to "cast your bread upon the waters," and it will return, as I've heard it said, "buttered on both sides." (See Ecclesiastes 11:1.)

I recently met a man who is one of the largest givers to my church. He told me that during the previous year he gave 70 percent of his income to the church. He was looking forward to the day when he could give 90 percent! He was putting all his available resources to use.

I told the story of how I gave my retirement fund to help build our church sanctuary, and then how my investment property shot up in value after the golf course went in. There's more to that story. A few years later our church needed an education building, and the Lord told me to give away the money I'd made from that property. So I went to my family again, and they agreed. We sold the land for $375,000 and helped the church build the education wing.

Our decision as a family was to put the money to use rather than to sit on it.

One of the main reasons I believe God has blessed my church is that we are an investing church. In 1994 when I was helping to get the Dream Center going, I made a decision not to give any money to the Dream Center. Instead we would give to missions elsewhere. We made that decision because, in a sense, the Dream Center was our baby church, and we knew that blessings come from giving money away to others, not to yourself.

So we continued to give money to missions— more than nine million dollars in a two-year period—the most of any church in our denomination. We didn't hoard the money for our own projects, but we injected it into other worthy ministries. And God provided all that the Dream Center needed through other people, churches and organizations.

I believe there are four levels of blessing when we give:

- The *bag* level

- The *barrel* level
- The *basket* level
- The *barn* level

Bag-level givers live in *hoard* mode. Consequently, they never have enough. Haggai 1:6 explains it well.

> You have planted much, but have harvested little. You eat, but never have enough. You drink, but never have your fill. You put on clothes, but are not warm. You earn wages, only to put them in a purse with holes in it.

When you hoard money, it's like storing it in a bag with holes. When you keep money a long time, the threads of the bag rot, the money falls to the ground and is lost. This is the kingdom consequence for keeping money or resources out of circulation.

The bag level is really *the beg level*. You don't have money for repairs, entertainment, clothes or extra things. Instead, you're barely scraping by, just living from one deposit to another. That's because the bag mentality is a "my" mentality. It's driven by selfishness. I can't help but think of Judas Iscariot. Because he was the treasurer of the disciples, he had a bag. He also had a bag mentality and grumbled when Jesus allowed Mary to "waste" money by anointing Him with expensive perfume.

In the end, Judas found himself holding another bag—one containing silver received in exchange for selling out Jesus. His act of betrayal was one of greed.

The bag mentality is motivated by a spirit of fear. But God wants us to sow even in times of famine and drought. We'll discover the barrel, basket and barn blessings as we continue looking at the ten things we can learn from Matthew 25.

### 6. WISE USE BRINGS INCREASE AND APPROVAL FROM GOD.

God approved of the faithful servants in Matthew 25 and told them to enter His joy. Increase makes God happy. He loves it when we use money wisely and are successful in His work.

> THE BAG MENTALITY IS MOTIVATED BY A SPIRIT OF FEAR.

The reason debt is so damaging is because it robs people of the opportunity to invest in the kingdom. Racking up debt is an unwise use of money. How can you give to missions when you're paying exorbitant finance charges on your credit card? How can you bless the kingdom when you mismanage your money? Some people are like a sieve—everything God gives them pours right through. They seem always to live on the edge, and it's no wonder. Even if God gave them more money, they would mismanage it and make it disappear.

Some people are impulsive spenders. We need to be impulsive givers!

But even in our impulsive giving, we need to be wise givers. I once heard a story about a woman named Oseola McCarty from Mississippi. She lived alone most of her life and survived by doing laundry for her neighbors. Because of family circumstances, she had dropped out of school after the sixth grade, and so she could never get a high-paying job. But in 1996 she gave $150,000 to the University of Southern Mississippi.

The local media heard what happened and ran a story. Then the national media picked it up, and articles about Oseola appeared in the *New York Times, Newsweek* and other publications. She was also given an honorary doctorate from Harvard University.[3]

## GOD LOVES IT WHEN WE USE MONEY WISELY AND ARE SUCCESSFUL IN HIS WORK.

Why so much hoopla? Because it is so rare for someone to give so generously. God approves of wise use of money, and He even helps us to celebrate!

Some people move from the bag mentality to a *barrel* mentality: They have enough to live on, with a little extra. When people give up the bag for the barrel, they are just learning to trust God. They are learning the truth of Philippians 4:19:

> And my God will meet all your needs according to his glorious riches in Christ Jesus.

The barrel mentality is the kindergarten stage. God proves He is your source, not your social security, your boss, your insurance or the stock market. You begin to relate to Psalm 37:25, which says:

> I was young and now I am old, yet I have never seen the righteous forsaken or their children begging bread.

The concept of the barrel comes from the story of Elijah and the famine. He stayed with a woman who had a barrel with a little grain in the bottom, and every time she scooped some out, there was still more. She had enough, and just a little left over.

> For this is what the LORD, the God of Israel, says: "The jar of flour will not be used up and the jug of oil will not run dry until the day the Lord gives rain on the land."
> —1 KINGS 17:14

When we begin to believe that God is our source, we graduate to barrel blessings.

### 7. A NEGATIVE ATTITUDE TOWARD GOD IS THE BASIS FOR MISUNDERSTANDING INVESTMENT.

If we don't have a right view of God, we won't have faith to invest. If we see God as a miser, we tend to become miserly, but if we see Him as having unlimited wealth, we are liberated to give. This is true for individuals—and for nations. Economy grows out of theology. America's economic principles grew out of our founders' understanding of God. The wealth of our country did not come from a belief in capitalism; it came from a correct view of God. With a correct view of God, we will know—and act upon—the belief that every man is a ruler under God and responsible for the resources with which God endows him. Our systems of enterprise and

entrepreneurship came from the religious beliefs
of the Puritans and pilgrims.

## GOD IS A JOYFUL
## INVESTOR, NOT A MEAN OVERSEER.

But during the twentieth century there was a
shift in our belief systems. Many Americans
began to hold the government responsible for
resources and for taking care of people. That
damaging "theology" could eventually wreck our
economy. It turns people into takers rather than
workers, hoarders instead of investors.

I'm praying that God restores the pioneer
spirit in America. Our faith should not be placed
in a government, but rather in our God-given
capacity to explore, invent and invest. The Bible
says, "If a man will not work, he shall not eat" (2
Thess. 3:10).

But if we have an accurate view of God, we are
eager to put what we have to use. God is a joyful
investor, not a mean overseer.

## 8. THOSE UNWILLING TO INVEST, GOD CALLED
## WICKED AND LAZY.

To not invest is a sin of wickedness, not just
neglect. People who sit on their money, not
willing to give or invest it and thinking they are
protecting God's assets, are actually wicked.
They are not prudent or wise as we might think.

Risk avoiders incur God's wrath. They fail to
reflect God's character. They don't recognize that
the value of money is not found in our capacity
to keep—it is found in our capacity to give.

By developing the capacity to give, the believer begins to reap the reward of *basket blessings*. You graduate to the basket level when you openly share what you have. You've gone beyond the kindergarten level of just barely being able to trust God to supply your basic needs. Now you are putting the principle to use. You are no longer wicked and lazy, a hoarder with a bag mentality. Now you have an open basket.

As a demonstration one time during a sermon, I carried a huge basket filled with chocolate chip cookies and jugs of iced tea down the aisles of the sanctuary to share with everyone. The people who showed up that Sunday got an extra treat!

Basket living says I've got enough for me and for you—no problem. Think of the boy who shared his loaves and fishes that day when Jesus miraculously multiplied the food for the hungry masses. (See Matthew 14:13–21.) That boy left the house with one basket of food and returned with twelve. Imagine the surprise of his mother as she washed the dishes and looked out the window and suddenly saw her son returning home—with twelve disciples in tow, each carrying a basket of loaves and fishes! When you share with others, there's always more left than what you started with.

If you refuse to share, not only are you being selfish—you are also wicked and lazy.

9. IF YOU FAIL TO USE WHAT GOD GIVES YOU, YOU LOSE OUT.

You've heard the phrase, "Use it or lose it."

That's how God works, according to this story.

There was a time when I could play the piano fairly well, but I haven't played in years. Now I've just about lost the ability altogether. I didn't use it, and I lost it.

Money is meant to be used. The only way to have more is to use what you have. If you don't, God will take what you have and give it to someone who will invest and take risks.

## 10. THOSE WHO HAVE WILL HAVE MORE.

Over the years, nine different people in our congregation have each given the church a million dollars. Why would they trust me with that money? I asked that question, and each giver told me the same thing: Because they know their money goes to reach the poor.

How do you get more? By investing! That's the only way to have anything—to give it away. The money was taken away from the servant who kept his investment safe by not giving it away. It may seem paradoxical, unfair, unjust, unwise and imprudent, but it's how the kingdom works. It is also how we must work if we are to function within the kingdom.

Those who learn to invest have moved up to the *barn level* of blessings. A barn is used for temporary storage. If you keep grain in it for too long, it spoils. But as long as grain flows in and out, it stays fresh.

Barns are symbolic of God's blessing when they are used correctly. In the Book of Genesis, Joseph was given the keys to the granaries of

Egypt because he kept himself pure and trust-worthy. God displayed His trust in Joseph by putting him in charge of big barns. Joseph knew when to store up and when to give out.

If Joseph had hoarded grain during the famine, judgment would have come upon Egypt. When wealth is not used correctly, judgment always comes on that wealth. God might allow you to accumulate wealth, but if you don't use it, you'll lose it.

The barn owner in Jesus' story in Luke 12 made a fatal mistake. He stopped the flow of grain through his barns and turned them into permanent storage facilities. Was it wrong for him to build big barns? No. Barns are meant to hold resources for a season. He was wicked because he stopped the flow.

## THE RETURN

What do we get when we give money away? We get a major return on the investment! I have tried throughout my life to give away more than God can give back to me, and I've failed every time. Every time I give, He gives back to me somehow. That doesn't mean I'm rich materially. It means God has given me a steady stream of money and resources to give away.

I've seen it happen for others, too.

A pastor named Dave Crone from Vacaville, California came to my pastor's school one year. In one of the services, I announced that I would be taking an offering for the Dream Center, asking pastors to sow into the miracle. But I didn't take the offering immediately. Instead I told them to think about what to give during that day and to come back that night prepared to give.

Crone climbed up the mountain outside our church to pray. Just a few days earlier his church had taken an offering to build a new building. They weren't able to borrow from the bank and needed to build using cash only. In that offering they raised $126,000, and that's all they had to get started on their building.

That day on the mountain the Lord spoke to him and said, "It's going to take $4 million to build your church in Vacaville; $126,000 is only a speck of what you need. Give all that you've raised so far to the Dream Center as a seed."

Of course, that put a lump in his throat! He had worked hard to raise that much. I've often heard this expression: When your need is bigger than what you have, make your need a seed. That is exactly what Crone decided to do. He didn't give the money that night because he needed to get permission from his church, so he went back to Vacaville and put it to a vote. He decided that unless he got 100 percent approval, he wouldn't give the money to the Dream Center. He made his case to the people of his church, and they voted unanimously to give the money. Crone gave me a check for $126,000. The Lord told him that by the end of that year he'd have $1 million to start his own building.

One year later Crone had $1 million to start, and two years later I dedicated their thirty-five-hundred-seat sanctuary—built debt free. That little $126,000 investment, which seemed so big at the time, came back to them pressed down, shaken together and running over.

## SURPRISE RETURNS

Crone learned a great lesson about generosity and faith. I learned that lesson in my own way when we were starting the Dream Center.

For years I have gone around the country helping pastors build their churches, giving them ideas and preaching in their services—even when I was so tired I could hardly stand. That generosity reaped great results when I needed money to kick-start the Dream Center. Many pastors I knew couldn't wait to give back.

Pastor George Sawyer from Alabama had attended my pastor's school for years. He built his church on our model, including Christmas and Easter pageants, buses and fireworks shows. His church had grown substantially.

He decided to start a Dream Center of his own. Someone gave him $10,000 to start with—the largest single gift he had ever received. But he also had a great desire to give to the original Dream Center in Los Angeles, so he decided to give that money to us. The Lord spoke to him and said, "You're not really sowing something from your congregation, because all that money came from one person. Ask your people what they want to give." They took an offering of $85,000! I preached there and received the check.

One year later a man in this pastor's church

realized a huge gain from an Internet business he sold. The businessman walked into the pastor's office and handed him a check for $1 million.

Another pastor from Oklahoma has one of the largest missions-giving churches in America. He patterned his ministry model after mine, putting on our illustrated sermons and holding a Fourth of July celebration just like ours. (He even set his grass on fire like we did!) For years he came to our pastor's school in Phoenix.

One year that pastor brought two men who toured the Dream Center and were so moved that they decided to give half a million dollars. Their gift came at a very desperate hour for the Dream Center. We were being forced by the city to bring the remaining floors in the center up to code. If we didn't do this, the city would shut us down.

I had sown into the life of this man for years. He has become a friend to me. Because of that investment of mine, I have seen it come back more than I could have imagined.

## LIQUOR MONEY?

When you realize that God is your source, you don't scramble around for money as if it's disappearing down rabbit holes. You don't worry about where it will come from.

A while ago I got a call from a man who organized golf tournaments. He wanted to make the Dream Center the beneficiary of the proceeds from an elite fund-raising golf tournament event in Los Angeles. A number of actors and well-known business leaders were going to participate in the celebrity golf tournament.

> GOD IS THE DREAM
> CENTER'S SOURCE—
> NOT A LIQUOR COMPANY
> OR A GOLF TOURNAMENT.

However, I learned that a liquor company was sponsoring the tournament. At first I thought of the scripture that says, "A sinner's wealth is stored up for the righteous" (Prov. 13:22). I was happy about that thought. But then the Holy Spirit pointed out to me that this liquor company would be attaching its bad name to our good name. The Spirit also reminded me that many of the people at the Dream Center were there because of problems with liquor.

I turned down the offer. Why? I did it because God is the Dream Center's source—not a liquor company or a golf tournament.

Mike Rogers first came to our Phoenix pastor's school in 1993. At the time he was a not-yet-successful businessman whose business debts outweighed his profits. He was a tither, but not a giver, and during the conference he realized that he was limiting God by holding so tightly to his money. One afternoon at the conference he prayed and asked God what God wanted him to give that night in the offering. The Lord told him $200, which was all he had in his wallet. It was scary for him, but he obeyed.

Mike came back to the pastor's school the next

year, where he heard about the Dream Center for the first time. Once again he asked God what he should give, and he felt that the Lord told him to give $100 a month above his tithe. That amount demanded more faith, but Mike was obedient.

The next year he prayed again, and the Lord told him to give $400 a month.

The next year it was $1,000 a month.

The year after that, God asked him to give $4,000 a month.

Each time God asked him to give more, Mike's obedience required that he overcome fear and be willing to sacrifice more. And the amount continued to grow—as did Mike's business. The next year it was $10,000 a month to the Dream Center; the next year, $17,000 a month; and then $21,000 a month. Most people can't imagine giving that kind of money in a year, let alone a month, but God was clearly putting it in Mike's hands for a purpose.

Last year Mike and his wife gave more than $400,000 to the Dream Center, above his regular tithe. They are debt free in their business and personal finances. His business, worth nothing in 1993, today is worth $50 million. Mike is now traveling and speaking on giving.

Why has God blessed them? Because they gave! They proved trustworthy with the dollars God put in their bank account.

## ENJOY YOUR MONEY!

After saying all that, I want to make it clear that I'm no killjoy. I don't advocate giving away so much that you neglect your own well-being. Money is for enjoyment, too. After you have given money to God and paid all your debts, live a little! Go on vacation. Rent a recreational vehicle. Go water skiing. Stay at a bed and breakfast. Buy the big mocha at Starbucks. Do something you enjoy. The Bible indicates that the Son of Man enjoyed His life (Matt. 11:19). Shouldn't we follow that example now and then?

A wealthy man in my church wanted to buy a Corvette but felt guilty about doing so. He asked my advice, and I told him, "Go buy the car! You're giving away most of your income already. Enjoy life." He bought a Corvette and took me for a ride. Wouldn't you know it, he put the pedal down a bit too much, and the police pulled him over—although they let him off without a ticket.

Everybody has a weakness for something—chocolate bonbons, leather bags, exotic neckties. My weakness is tennis shoes. When I walk through the mall I can hardly pass up a pair of athletic shoes if I see them in a store window. I probably have eight pairs of shoes—for walking, jumping, running, playing basketball. I know I don't need them, but at times I can't resist.

It's OK to treat yourself well, to enjoy life as Jesus did, to celebrate when it's time to celebrate as long as we learn the other side as well:

> It is more blessed to give than to receive.
> —ACTS 20:35

As I've given money away through the years, God has continued giving to me. But the returns are not always monetary. I have things money can't buy—two sons pastoring great churches; a daughter whose husband, a successful businessman, is a great supporter of Phoenix First; and five wonderful grandchildren.

It's true: When you learn to give money away, God will reward your investment with greater wealth and with riches that can't be measured in dollars and cents.

The same is true when we give away other things, as we'll see in coming chapters.

# SIX

# BOUNDLESS ENERGY

In 1997 I embarked on a four-hundred-mile run from Phoenix to Los Angeles to raise money for the Dream Center. I wrote about that experience in my book *Adventure Yourself*—about the sores on my feet and phlebitis in my legs and the many times I didn't think I could go on because my body wanted to give up. Then there was the triumphant finish, the celebration and the support raised for our ministry. The run, completed twenty-six miles at a time over the course of two weeks, was one of the highlights of my life.[1]

But in the year after the run, I got lazy. I had heard that marathon runners rested one day for every mile they ran, meaning they rested twenty-six days after each marathon. I had run twenty-six miles on nineteen days, so I figured I had at least a year off! It was a self-serving rationalization.

After a year or so I began to see the effects of inactivity. I gained weight, had less energy and was not nearly as fit as before. I knew I had a challenge ahead of me to get back in shape. I had so many dreams and goals of seeing the Dream Center spread around the world that I needed to make my body last!

Several new buildings were being constructed near my house, and one of them turned out to be a fitness center. Whenever I drove by I thought about joining, and one day I made the decision to change my habits. I took the money I normally spent on golf and put it toward joining the gym. Golf doesn't do much for your physical health, but working out does.

I took it one step further and got a personal trainer. I was sixty-three years old at the time, and it was the first time I'd lifted weights or worked with a trainer. Oh, the difference it makes! I meet with my trainer three mornings a week, and he takes me through an hour-long regimen of weightlifting. It's hard and not very pleasant! By the end I'm sweating and huffing and puffing. The trainer pushes me to do the exercises correctly, to keep a quick pace and to challenge myself with more weights and different exercises. He's like a drill sergeant, especially when he makes me do stomach exercises like sit-ups, which I have never liked.

What I do like is the energy the exercise gives me. By giving away energy I have more energy than ever. I don't like giving the energy. I don't enjoy exercise, but I'm stronger than I've ever been. I sleep better, I have better posture and a clearer mind, and I can accomplish more physically and mentally because of a heightened energy level and sense of focus.

I love going home and showing my wife the muscles in my arms. "Look how much my muscles have grown!" I brag. And I get a little kick out of telling people, "I worked out today!"

## USE IT OR LOSE IT

If I didn't give energy, I wouldn't get energy. When bodies are used, they last longer. The people who think they are "conserving" their bodies by not exercising are missing the point. Only by using the energy we have can we gain more energy.

> IF WE'RE GOING TO GIVE OUR TIME AND MONEY AWAY, WE SHOULD ALSO GIVE OUR ENERGY AWAY.

Think about buying a brand-new car and then leaving it in the garage for thirty years. It may have only ten miles on it, but you won't be able to start it up. The parts will have aged and corroded; many may need replacing.

If you have ever left a car for a couple of weeks while away on vacation, you know that inactivity brings out the worst in it. For example, if you have a slow battery leak, two weeks is enough to drain the battery entirely. What a surprise when you try to start it up in the morning to go to work, and the engine just clicks. But if you are driving the car every day, the engine recharges the battery.

That's how it is with humans. God rewards work. He rewards the expenditure of energy. Astronauts have found that the longer they stay in no-gravity environments, the weaker they become. Their muscles atrophy very quickly. Their bones become brittle. Their immune system becomes considerably weaker.

Why? It seems to go against logic. After all, with no gravity to pull on your body and stress it out, it makes sense that we would live longer. Space would seem to be the best environment for long life.

But the opposite is true. Our bodies need resistance to prod them to grow. That's what weightlifting is all about—tearing the muscles so they rebuild in stronger fashion.

If we're going to give our time and money away, we should also give our energy away. The only way to gain strength is by giving energy. It's another paradox of kingdom living, but it actually works.

## BLESSED ARE THE DOERS

There are some people who feel guilty about "wasting" time on exercise or recreation. I have a rule about exercise and leisure: If it makes me a better Christian, then it's good. If it makes me more relaxed and improves my mind, attitude and health, if it helps me do more for God, then it's right.

Let me take this principle a little further and show you how it applies to our spiritual lives. Some Christians are stuck in neutral, all the while praying for God to give them direction. They are praying for energy without giving energy.

One of my favorite bits of advice is this: If you're not moving ahead, the Bible has nothing to say to you about guidance.

We have to get the order right. Spend energy first, and then see what God does.

Consider Abraham. He expended energy before knowing where he was going. God gave him directions only after he was on his way. He was so unlike some of the people who say to me, "I've been waiting around for a word from God about what I should do."

My advice for them—and you, "Here's a word for you. Go!"

SPEND ENERGY FIRST, AND
THEN SEE WHAT GOD DOES.

Even 1 percent of *doing* is worth more than 100 percent of *intending to do*. Jesus said, "Now that you know these things, you will be blessed if you do them" (John 13:17). He didn't say, "If you know it or hear it." The best thing to do if you're stuck in neutral is to give energy to something, even if it's not the exact thing God wants you to do. I guarantee that once you get started, He'll show you the right way.

One time a man came to me after a pastor's conference in Davenport and said, "You've given us all these principles, but I want to know the real secret to how you got your church to grow. I know you've held something back."

"You really want to know?" I asked. "Come with me into the back room. I don't want anyone else to hear." We went to the back room, and I said, "Put your ear close to my mouth. I don't want anyone to hear this secret." Then I yelled as loud as I could, "Work!"

His eyes got big, and he was a little bit confused. He wanted to latch on to some secret that would allow him to avoid giving too much energy, but that's not the way it works.

The Bible testifies time and again to the power of doing. Genesis 1:1 says, "In the beginning God created…" The beginning point was when He *did* something. It doesn't say, "In the beginning God considered." The start of the thing was with the action, not the consideration.

In Genesis 11:6 the people of the world began building the tower of Babel.

> The LORD said, "If as one people speaking the same language they have begun to do this, then nothing they plan to do will be impossible for them."

Once you get started, nothing will be impossible for you. That's the power of energy. With our finite energy, we can invite infinite resources. That's an incredible equation!

To *do* is to expend energy. That's not always comfortable or appealing to us, but it's the only way to gain more physical and spiritual vibrancy.

## ADDING RESISTANCE

The only way to continually add strength is to add more resistance. In life, the only way to grow is to have resistance, trials and problems. Perhaps that's why James started his New Testament letter with these words:

> Consider it pure joy, my brothers, whenever you face trials of many kinds, because you know that the testing of your faith develops perseverance.
>
> —JAMES 1:2

Many people have goals or dreams, but sometimes the goal seems too lofty to be real, so they scale back and shoot for something manageable. That's not the right way to grow.

You grow by becoming equal to a task that is bigger than you. To become a better Christian, take on more responsibility and more work, and you will grow into greatness. None of us are miracle workers, but all of us can be miracles. We become a miracle by taking on more than we can handle.

## FROM VESSEL TO VESSEL

One of the ways in which God gets us to spend energy is by allowing trouble to visit us. People can be like a horse that won't get started until he feels the spurs in his ribs.

> YOU GROW BY BECOMING EQUAL TO A TASK THAT IS BIGGER THAN YOU.

In Jeremiah 48, the Bible describes the condition of Moab shortly before its destruction:

> Moab has been at rest from youth, like wine

> left on its dregs, not poured from one jar to
> another—she has not gone into exile. So she
> tastes as she did, and her aroma is unchanged.
> —JEREMIAH 48:11

This passage describes the difference between a hothouse flower and a tough outside plant. The flower dies as soon as adversity hits, but the outside plant has been strengthened by regular troubles.

It also describes the condition of someone who doesn't change. His *taste* and *aroma*—meaning his personality and character—remain the same. Change can be painful, but it adds character.

One of the ways any church stays strong over a long period of time is by facing adversity and triumphing over it. My own church remains strong, healthy and growing because of the battles we've fought regularly. Expending that energy was similar to my workouts—it helped us to stay strong and lean as a congregation. When a church is regularly poured from vessel to vessel, losing the dregs, it gets stronger.

## CHANGE CAN BE PAINFUL,
## BUT IT ADDS CHARACTER.

---

I also see this principle at work in my own life in the struggles I faced trying to develop a ministry. First I had to convince people to ask a sixteen-year-old evangelist to speak in their churches. When I ran buses in Davenport, people said all I had was a bunch of snot-nosed kids, and they accused me of merely playing the "numbers game."

Later, in Phoenix, I fought to turn the church

from a sort of complacent, status-quo group of people who just wanted to grow quietly in their faith into an outreach-loving church.

There were battles about the use of our church property, and at one point I was unfairly portrayed in a national newspaper.

This is not a pity party—far from it. The truth is, I'm grateful for these trials, and I'm very aware that my trials are no greater than anyone else's. I see now that I grew stronger then—and became more like a tough weed and less like a delicate flower.

To be used by God, you have to have a lifetime of being poured from vessel to vessel. It makes you work, hustle and put forth effort.

My son Luke recently went to pastor a church in Ohio, and under his leadership it grew from one hundred seventy-five to over six hundred in a short period of time. I had counseled him not to go because I had a hunch there would be problems with the old pastor who had been there for forty-seven years and legally "owned" the church. Sure enough, the doors were locked on Luke, and he had no place to go but to the Holiday Inn to hold services. His congregation moved from place to place. At one point he called me and said, "Dad, when is all this trouble going to stop?" I didn't have the heart to tell him that troubles of that sort would last a lifetime!

But I also knew God was pouring him from vessel to vessel, making him stronger.

Everybody has stories to tell. My own mother was beaten by her stepfather. She still has bad hearing from the time he slapped her on the side of the head.

My wife was born in Helsinki, Finland during the winter wars with the Russians, and her father was killed in that war. Famine came, and her mother turned to the streets to sell her body to buy food. Even then it wasn't enough. Finally, with rickets and a bloated stomach, at age fourteen my future wife was shipped off to be adopted in Sweden! Eventually she came to America, hoping to find a husband and a normal life. She found me, and I found her, and I saw that this woman's strength came from being poured from vessel to vessel.

## IT'S A BUMPY ROAD

As a young man I had the opportunity to hear Lee Roberson, a great preacher and pastor of a large Baptist church in Chattanooga, Tennessee. One night he announced that he was going to preach on "What Makes Men Great."

TO BE USED BY
GOD, YOU HAVE
TO HAVE A LIFETIME OF BEING
POURED FROM VESSEL TO VESSEL.

I was beside myself with anticipation. To me, it was a golden opportunity to hear from a great man what made his ministry, his life, so much above normal. I wanted to be great for God, too. I arrived early and sat on the front row with my pad and pen ready.

That night Roberson came onto the platform when it was time to preach and announced again that he was going to tell us what makes men great. He told us to get ready to write it down and commit it to memory. My pen hovered over the paper, my ears tingling. Then he spoke.

"What makes men great?" he said. "Here it is: *Trouble.*"

Then he turned and walked off the platform! That was the whole service.

Adversity makes men great. Our greatest presidents—the ones we find on our coinage and dollar bills—were the ones who presided over our country during her greatest times of trouble. Abraham Lincoln, George Washington, Thomas Jefferson—each faced a crisis that literally threatened any chance of success. At one time or another, each of these men was called a failure.

But that adversity proved to be the foundation of their greatness. And I'm sure that along the way they decided to enjoy the difficulties instead of complaining.

I once read that many of our presidents could have been great, but we will never know of their greatness because they never had adversity in their administration. I write this in the aftermath of the September 11, 2001 terrorist attacks, and I can't help but think that President George W. Bush has been handed a chance to be great because of the crisis that befell our country under his watch. Presidents who preside over prosperity tend to be forgotten. Who remembers the presidents of the roaring twenties, a decade of unparalleled prosperity, much like the 1990s were? Nobody remembers those presidents or their administrations, but we all remember FDR because he took our nation through depression and war.

No president can choose the adversity he will face, and neither can we, but we should get used to it and accept it as a pattern of life.

One day as I drove from Phoenix to Flagstaff, road repairs forced me to take a detour. Suddenly I hit a bump. I thought it was the only one, but there came another bump and then another. I realized this wasn't a bump in the road—it was a bumpy road. I could be annoyed about it, or I could learn to enjoy it.

IT'S NOT THE PROTECTED,
PAMPERED PERSON
WHO PLEASES GOD—
IT'S THE ONE WHO USES
HIS GOD-GIVEN ENERGIES
TO OVERCOME CHALLENGES.

The bumpy road made me think about my career as a young pastor. When I first started I seemed to hit bumps once a month. Then they started coming once a week, and now they seem to come every hour! But I don't see those bumps as miserable interruptions anymore—I see them as God-given challenges meant to strengthen me. It's not just a bump in the road—it's a bumpy road, and I delight in the fact that I can take the bumps.

All who live in Jesus will suffer, but the Lord will raise them up. That's the way life is. It's not the protected, pampered person who pleases God—it's the one who uses his God-given energies to overcome challenges. Eventually, like Paul, we can actually make light of our infirmities.

# SEVEN

# HOW TO HAVE UNLIMITED LOVE

I remember the evening in Palo Alto, California when I met the love of my life.

Her name was Marja, and she came from Sweden. She couldn't speak English well, but she was one of the most gorgeous people I had ever seen.

I was holding a revival at what had been my uncle's church, one of the largest churches in the state. It sat right next to Stanford University. My uncle had been killed when a train hit his car. It was a devastating thing to the church, and my aunt asked me, a twenty-seven-year-old evangelist, to pastor the church until they found a permanent replacement. I was there for three months.

The service went well that night, and as I prayed for people at the altar I noticed Marja, this extremely beautiful blond woman, kneeling at the altar. She had answered the call to salvation. I was captivated and made my way slowly, unassumingly over to where she was kneeling so I could pray for her!

After the service we introduced ourselves and began to talk. She was in America to attend flight attendant school so she could work for an airline. To support herself she worked as a nanny for wealthy people in the Bay Area. The more we talked, the more I wanted to spend time with her, but I was unsure whether or not I should. As an evangelist, for the ten years up to that point I wouldn't allow myself to date because I didn't want people to think I was coming to town just to find a pretty girl. But as the pastor of this church, I felt a little more freedom. And I couldn't resist Marja's beauty and grace.

I got up my courage and asked her out on a date, and for three months we saw each other regularly. Then I asked her to marry me. I was elated, but our backgrounds were so different that we should have known we would face challenges. She grew up in a very liberal culture in Sweden, had little familiarity with American culture and even less with Pentecostal churches. Her family was Lutheran, her father an atheist.

I was from the Midwest and grew up in fiery Pentecostal churches. I knew nothing of Swedish culture.

But we were young and full of optimism, so we went ahead with our engagement. I was getting ready to go overseas for three months on a preaching tour, so we decided she would stay with my parents in Kansas City and learn about the ministry, and then we would be married when I got home. Those months were rough on her as she began to learn what being a pastor's wife was like, but when I returned she was still committed to me and I to her, and we were married.

## TRYING TIMES

From the start, there was tension. We started fighting on our honeymoon, and when we returned and went together on the evangelistic field, it got harder. At the time, Pentecostal women didn't wear make-up, especially in church, and anyone who did was considered worldly. Marja had never heard of such a rule. She was from an entirely different culture. At one point she had finished as the runner-up in the Miss Sweden contest—that's how beautiful she was. But I knew how legalistic Pentecostal people could be, so every night before church I would make her take her make-up off. That would always lead to a fight. Then, each time I gave the altar call at the end of the service, she would respond and "get saved" again because she was so new to Christianity and felt the conviction of the Holy Spirit.

I decided that if my marriage was going to last I would have to quit the evangelistic field for a while. I stopped booking preaching engagements and became an associate at my dad's church in Kansas City, getting paid $100 a week—not enough to pay our bills. Marja and I lived behind the church in a parsonage. During the day I worked for a tree-trimming service, and in the afternoon I worked in an auto store selling cans of oil. Sometimes during those long hours I would think back to what I'd had just a few years before. I had been a successful evangelist and preached in some of the largest arenas in America and around the world. Now here I was, cutting tree branches, coming home with my arms scraped up, then going to the auto shop. At night I assisted my father in his church, and God really did move while we were there. We were having genuine revival, and the people of the church were compassionate and understanding toward Marja and me.

## AS I WATCHED HER GO, I CRIED LIKE A BABY, THINKING MY MINISTRY AND MARRIAGE WERE OVER.

But our relationship had deteriorated to the point that we no longer felt the emotional excitement of being together that we felt when we first met. I had married a girl who hadn't been exposed to Christianity for long. She had chosen me and agreed to serve God with me. I had dragged her into a life she didn't understand and didn't like. She hated having to stick to religious rules, hated playing a part that didn't feel natural to her. On top of all that, she felt imprisoned because she was still learning English.

There was a time in our marriage when the strain was so great that I wondered if we'd ever make it as husband and wife. I especially doubted if she could handle being a pastor's wife. We seemed to be at an impasse. She could not get used to the demands of the ministry and the peculiar, restrictive environment of Pentecostalism, and I couldn't have her running around with make-up on. Then there were the hundreds of differences, big and small, that arose because of our different backgrounds.

In just two months we were ready to end our marriage. I knew I was responsible for the entire mess. I had made my choice, and now I had to sort through the consequences. One day, by mutual agreement, I took Marja to the airport and put her on a plane to go to California to stay with a girlfriend there. As I watched her go, I cried like a baby, thinking my ministry and marriage were over.

But a few hours later, the phone rang at our house. It was Marja. She was in California, but her attitude had changed—and by this time so had mine. She said she knew it wasn't right to leave. We apologized to each other, and I told her to come back and we would make it work. She got on a plane the next day, and I picked her up at the airport. There still were no feelings, no enthusiasm for the uphill battle we faced, but what we didn't know was that we were taking the first steps on a journey toward true love.

## IMPRISONED SPLENDOR

Giving love is one of the most difficult things to do. In many ways it's more difficult than giving money, because love has to come from an open heart. There's no way to make it a cold business transaction.

But many of us misunderstand what love is. We think it's something that we can receive and possess, like a gift or something owed. But that's not what love really is. Love is something you can only *give*, not something you possess. None of us *own* love—we *use* love. The Bible word for love is in the active tense, meaning that love ungiven is not love at all.

## WE DON'T NEED
## TO BE LOVED AS MUCH
## AS WE NEED TO LOVE SOMEONE.

Have you ever met people who seem to be like a black hole when it comes to love—always pulling it in, but never getting enough? The more they focus on the love they feel they deserve, the less love they seem to have. They are so focused on their lack that their supply is never enough.

I speak with people all the time who tell me they just want to be loved by someone. I have discovered that the opposite is true: *We don't need to be loved as much as we need to love someone.* When we love unconditionally, we can never become imprisoned to a man or woman. But when we demand that somebody love us, we become their slave and are easily imprisoned by their lack of love toward us.

I honestly believe it's more important for people to show love than to receive it. When you show love, it turns on the heavenly faucet from which God pours love continually into us. The more love you show, the more you have and the easier it is to leave the tap on and let it flow to others.

People can be so focused on getting someone else's love that they don't see the love already inside them. The Bible says, "The kingdom of God is within you"—not without you (Luke 17:21). The love is already there! The poet Robert Browning spoke of "imprisoned splendor," a beautiful phrase.[1] He meant that the love of the kingdom is already within us, but it's imprisoned. The trick is getting it to flow from us to others. Jesus often spoke about the kingdom of God, teaching us that it began within us and flowed out to others.

> Do not be afraid, little flock, for your Father has been pleased to give you the kingdom.
> —LUKE 12:32

> Whoever drinks the water I give him will never thirst. Indeed, the water I give him will become in him a spring of water welling up to eternal life.
> —JOHN 4:14

> If anyone is thirsty, let him come to me and drink. Whoever believes in me, as the Scripture has said, streams of living water will flow from within him.
> —JOHN 7:37

It was Christ's desire that we recognize this flow of the kingdom of God from within one believer to others as having the power to give us fullness of life.

> I have come that they may have life, and have
> it to the full.
> —JOHN 10:10

Jesus is the source, and that living water is inside of us. God is not to blame for our lack of love. He can't possibly give us any more love than He offers already!

Then why are some so depressed? Mopey? Weighed down? Why do they feel that nobody loves them? They feel that way because they need to release the imprisoned splendor within them. It is so important that we catch the meaning of what Solomon wrote:

> Cast your bread upon the waters, for after
> many days you will find it again.
> —ECCLESIASTES 11:1

You can't get bread back until you've thrown it on the water. You can't get love until you give it away. If you will find a way to release that "imprisoned splendor," it will come back multiplied.

The amount of love you have is directly influenced by how much love you give. It's a paradox, but it's true: The only way to hold on to love is to give it away.

If you constantly give love away, you are always focused on what you have to give, and that supply will grow. Even if no one loves you back, you will have an endless supply of love through Jesus, and your life will be full of love.

## RELEASE THE LOVE YOU HAVE

A young man came up to me recently and asked

me to lay hands on him and impart to him the love I have for people. I told him that I couldn't impart love; only the Holy Spirit can do that. But I promised him that one day he would love greatly if only he would love as much as he loved right now.

What I meant was this: The path to great love begins with using the love you already have. You can't get great love in one giant step, and there is no shortcut. Love increases through the process of giving it away.

When I was young, I loved people less than I do now. But I tried giving love away and found that my own supply expanded. As long as I keep using the love I have, God continues giving me deeper love.

THE ONLY WAY TO HOLD
ON TO LOVE IS TO GIVE IT AWAY.

---

As a young man, I didn't love little children—I only tolerated them. But one day I made a choice to love them. Today my heart overflows with love for little children. I can say now that I genuinely love and enjoy children.

I enjoy life now, but when I was a young preacher I wasn't nearly as joyful. I have ten times the joy now that I did ten years ago. I made up my mind that I could choose to be dreary or joyful, and I may as well choose joy. To my surprise, I have found more joy coming to me since I decided to give it away.

You don't really get to know the Bible by merely reading it. But when you begin to teach it

to your children, or you take on teaching a
Sunday school class, then God's Word opens up
to you in ways you never knew before. It takes
practicing the Word by giving it to others. It's
the same way with love—it takes practicing it.

I'm reminded of the following poem:

> A bell is not a bell until you ring it.
> A song is not a song until you sing it.
> Love in your heart is not put there to stay;
> Love is not love until you give it away.[2]

## A RESTORED RELATIONSHIP

I learned volumes about love during those difficult early years of marriage after Marja returned
from California. We still didn't like each other,
let alone love each other, but we were forced to
find a way to make it work. Neither of us
believed in divorce, and we knew God wanted us
to stay together.

Little by little I began to see that pursuing love
was the wrong way to go about it. The more I
tried to get Marja to love me and make me
happy, the more miserable we both were. Trying
to grasp love was like trying to hold on to a
shadow.

Slowly I realized that to have love, you don't
seek it—you give it. Instead of measuring how
much love your spouse gives you, you simply
decide to love her (or him) no matter what, and
you seek to make her (or him) happy. Then a
marvelous change takes place. Your love is
released. The imprisoned splendor Browning
talked about breaks through the prison walls,

and you begin to have love and happiness from seeing your spouse happy.

Suddenly, you are not a slave to someone else. Your love comes from within, from the endless supply of kingdom love.

Today, I have the most blessed and enjoyable marriage a man could ask for. I love Marja unreservedly, and she loves me the same way. There was a time when sheer commitment kept us together, but now there aren't two people who love each more sincerely than we do.

> LOVE DOESN'T COME
> FROM ANY PERSON—
> IT COMES FROM GOD.

The contrast still amazes me. Today I look out when I'm preaching, and Marja is there, lifting her hands during worship. She visits hospitals and loves every aspect of the ministry. In all her years as a pastor's wife, she has never had a confrontation with a person in any of our congregations. Now the women flock to her to learn from her wisdom. She is, as a local newspaper once put it, "The Model Pastor's Wife"—a title playing off her background as a beauty queen, but far surpassing a beauty queen's influence!

And I have learned that my love doesn't come from any person—it comes from God. My love for Marja is pure because I found the source. I learned it is more blessed to give love than to receive it. Now I can thank God for those years and the pain we went through because it taught me that love is meant to be given, not taken.

## TAMALES AND KISSES

I have applied that principle to other people as well. I try to give love away whenever I can to my friends, my staff and my congregation. Usually when a church becomes as large as Phoenix First, the pastor is harder to find. He may surround himself with associates and handlers and make a point of ducking into back doors before people can get to him.

Fortunately, I don't have that kind of relationship with my people. I enjoy being with them, and I rarely feel too busy to love them. I stand at the door of our church every Sunday morning after preaching my heart out for two services, and for an hour I shake hands, hug necks and talk with little girls and boys, with young men in earrings and old people in wheelchairs. I love on all kinds of people.

One man came to church with an entirely negative attitude. He didn't like the music, the preaching or anything. But on the way out I hugged his neck, and he wrote me later to say, "What the music and the preaching couldn't do, your hug did." He came back and got saved!

We have a group of girls at the Dream Center who were once prostitutes. When they first came, they wouldn't look you in the eye but stood there with their heads down. After we poured love into them for months and months, they began to love people back. They stand in line to see me after every service, and as I hug each one of them, their eyes sparkle.

Every week I tell my congregation in Phoenix that I love them. They know I do, but people need to hear it regularly. And as I give away my love, I am loved. As I speak from the pulpit, I even have to be careful what I mention that I might want—because people try to give me whatever I mention. If I say I like steak, people just about run a herd of steer onto the stage.

I make a point of putting love within people's reach. Not everybody has the money to give big gifts, and I don't want big gifts anyway. So I talk about the foods I like—hot tamales, for instance, and candy Kisses and oatmeal cookies and bubble gum. Anybody can give those things, and they do. I get so many gifts of Kisses and hot tamales that I could paper my walls with wrappers from the Kisses and the tamale husks.

Why? Because I'm putting love within people's reach.

## LANGUAGE OF LOVE

People speak different love languages. Many times I counsel with a young person who doesn't think his or her father loves him. However, in reality that father loves his child more than anything, but he just hasn't found the right way to show it.

There are so many ways to show love. Some people show love by hugging and touching. They see each child as a candidate for a great big bear hug that makes the child's eyes pop out.

They pat people on the back, caress their necks, squeeze their arms and sit close to the people they love.

Other people are talkers and show love by saying they love you. If it's not verbal, it's not love to them. They have to speak it and hear it spoken.

Some show love by serving and teaching. They take you to school, do the laundry, buy the groceries. They're always volunteering for some task. If they don't "do," it's not love.

Some, particularly the breadwinners in families, show love by providing. They think that by earning the money they are showing love. They are happy to give to a friend in need, and that is their highest expression of love.

Some show love by giving gifts. When they feel love well up within them, they head to the mall to buy a gift for someone. They love Christmas and birthdays, and they spend money to show love.

Some show love by giving opportunities and adventures, especially to their children. My dad was that way. He shipped us off to have great experiences and memories we would remember. We didn't just go to Disneyland for vacation; my father loaded us up for a trip to Mexico City every summer. Our first stop was Laredo, then a resort in Monterey where we climbed to the waterfalls and looked at all the banana trees and monkeys. Then we drove into the mountains where we gave candy to kids who had never seen American candy. It seems that every time that was the stop where my family all caught the don't-drink-the-water flu.

Yet my dad would say, "Isn't this great?" He loved us by giving us great adventures.

When I was nine years old, he decided to give me a new adventure. He put me on a train from our home in Kansas City for a trip to Texas. My granddad picked me up at the train station, and for two months all I saw were rattlesnakes, scorpions and coyotes. We had to haul water from the city. That adventure was an example of my father loving me, and it gave me memories that last.

Others express love by giving large amounts of time. Kids call it *hanging out*. Some people live to spend time with the people they love. They carve out big chunks of time and set it aside because that's their way of showing love.

The challenge is figuring out which language your loved ones speak. Every person yearns to feel treasured in a unique way. Conventional wisdom says to treat everyone equally— including children. That way no one can claim they had special treatment. But that's not Bible wisdom. The Bible encourages us to love people in the special way they need it.

I've learned volumes about this from my children. My own style is to tell a child I love him and hug him to death. I also like to provide adventures and fun vacations, but I'm less interested in giving time or gifts.

But I've changed. As I've studied my children I've found they each have a language of love.

Luke needs to be told he's loved. He needs to be touched and patted on the back. He also likes adventures. He's easy for me to communicate with because we speak the same love language. I say it, and he feels it. I hug him; he gets it. I give him an adventure opportunity, and that clicks with him.

## THE CHALLENGE IS FIGURING OUT WHICH LANGUAGE YOUR LOVED ONES SPEAK.

Matthew is completely different. He was harder for me to figure out. His number one way of showing love is to spend time together. Lots of time. Slow-paced, crawling time. He likes long, slow conversations. But that was my most undeveloped way of conveying love. When he lived at home, Matthew would say things like, "Let's stay home tonight, kick back and chill out." One thing I'm not is laid back, and "chill out" to me means I need to put on a coat. Spending long times together was new ground for me because I had never been given long drawn-out attention from my dad. That wasn't the way he showed love.

But I've learned that language because I didn't want Matthew to grow up incomplete or scarred. I put my love in a language he understood, and I actually came to like slow-paced conversations. I began to crave that time spent with him, and I realized I had a need I didn't know about before. Learning that language opened up emotions I didn't know I had.

Then there's my daughter, Kristie, whom I jokingly call *my pearl of great price*. She likes to be told she's loved, likes to be hugged, but that doesn't ring her bells. She likes adventures, but that's not her language, either. If you want to convince Kristie you love her, you buy her gifts. I like to tell people that her favorite scripture is, "Where your treasure is, there your heart will be also" (Luke 12:34)!

She doesn't demand big things, and she's not materialistic, but love to her is tangible. Birthdays and other gift-giving holidays thrill her. She will even celebrate the Fourth of July as if it were a birthday! On the day after her birthday she used to tell us, "Only 364 days until my next birthday."

Once again, I had to learn to go against my nature. As a boy, my family rarely gave gifts, even on birthdays. We'd sing "Happy birthday to you," and that was it. So having a gift-loving girl was a challenge for me. I used to hate going through shopping malls—I often said I'd rather go through the Tribulation. But because I love her with all my heart, I changed. I learned to enjoy buying gifts because it meant so much to her.

Now I look forward to Kristie's birthdays. One of my joys is taking her down to the mall to buy her a gift. I didn't know I was the gift-giving type, but I have discovered I am. I was retarded in that way emotionally. Now I've developed that a little more.

We need to crawl out of our comfort zones and, by learning their love languages, learn to love in a way that our kids, spouse and friends can understand.

## WHO WILL LOVE?

There are a lot of skateboarders in Los Angeles and in the Dream Center's neighborhood. Famous skater Tony Hawk came to a nearby location to film a movie, and they built a huge half-pipe, reportedly the second largest in America, to use in the movie. Stella, our youth director, went down to watch the filming. She asked the producers what they were going to do with the $50,000-half-pipe when they were finished. They scratched their heads and said they didn't know. "But if you can move it, you can have it," they told her.

When they finished the filming, a bunch of guys from the Dream Center took the half-pipe apart and moved it to the center. Every Saturday we open it for skaters, but to get a ticket, each skater has to come to a service during the week. Every weekend, several hundred people come to skate that beautiful half-pipe, sitting in the parking lot next to the freeway in the shadow of the LA skyline.

That's a way of loving people—understanding their desires and helping to fulfill them. We thought, *Who else is going to be kind to these skaters out on the streets?* I believe our investment is making a difference in their lives.

When I first came to Los Angeles I purposed

to build the kind of church I built in Phoenix, one with a two-hundred-voice, white-robed choir and orchestra in black suits. I intended to sing songs on Sunday like "It Is Well With My Soul" and "How Great Thou Art"—songs I liked.

> WE NEED TO CRAWL
> OUT OF OUR COMFORT ZONES
> AND, BY LEARNING THEIR LOVE
> LANGUAGES, LEARN TO LOVE
> IN A WAY THAT OUR KIDS, SPOUSE
> AND FRIENDS CAN UNDERSTAND.

But when we did sing those songs, our young inner-city crowd went to sleep. Those songs were unknown and boring to them. Finally, one of the young people asked, "Can we just try our music once?" I agreed they could at the next service. When I walked into that auditorium next Sunday, guitars were wailing, bongos were beating, cymbals were crashing and the sound was so loud that insects were dying in the atmosphere and blood was pouring out of people's ears. As I listened to their song, I realized it was the old rock-and-roll hit "My Girl." The words had been changed to "My Lord." I thought, *My Lord, they're singing "My Girl" in church!*

When I asked the musicians about it, their response was, "Yes, but we got the song saved."

That night I decided that the *message* of the gospel was sacred—not the *method*. I had to admit there was an anointing on "My Lord" that night. We never went back to the old songs I liked. Now our singers and musicians are writing their own songs, creating their own style, and when I'm out traveling I hear their music all over the country.

We decided to "love" our crowd by singing in a way they could appreciate.

Who else is going to love people if not those of us in the family of God? Everyone else is targeting people with advertisements, bank offers, credit card offers, commercials or magazines. Did you know that corporate America has even divided the population into categories so they know how to market products? Here are some of the categories of the American population:

- *Up and Comers*—young, optimistic, childless couples who are actively making a name and bank account for themselves and their future families.
- *Young Materialists*—cynical, aggressive singles who think money equals happiness.
- *Stressed by Life* group—parents with not enough money and too many responsibilities.
- *New Traditionalists*—wealthy, family-oriented people who value community above all.
- The *Family Limiteds*—who are happily absorbed by the demands of family life and care about nothing else.
- *Detached Introverts*—the socially inept.
- *Renaissance Elders*—active senior citizens with lots of money to spend.

- The *Retired From Life* group—these have withdrawn from modern society and are suspicious of new technologies and ideas.[3]

That's how the marketers see us—as breathing bank accounts.

The people in this world need someone to love them! The cry of our day is for a bolder love. Many of us have known Christ for a long time, and yet His love is still imprisoned within us. He wants us to be conduits—not reservoirs. Some of us freeze up when we start to express love. We hold back our words because we fear expressing emotions.

## WHO ELSE IS GOING TO LOVE PEOPLE IF NOT THOSE OF US IN THE FAMILY OF GOD?

Some say, "My love won't mean much to that person, so I may as well keep it to myself." Yet every time someone expresses bold love to me, it melts me. Why wouldn't it do the same to others?

Others say, "What if I'm awkward and don't express it right?" I've had people start to tell me they love me and then get nervous and stammer. It makes me love them all the more! You can't mess up love. A heart of love comes through no matter what the words say.

One time a high school boy made an appointment to see me. When he arrived I asked him what he would like. He started to stammer and turn red. His words were all garbled, but he clearly wanted to say something that was on his heart. After a few painful minutes of not even completing a sentence, he blurted out, "Pastor, I love you!" Then he got up and ran out of my office!

I ran after him and asked, "Have you ever told someone you loved him?"

He said, "No, I never did."

It's not good enough to *feel* love for someone. You have to *show and tell* them. Love without expression is useless. It wrecks people's hearts not to know they are loved.

## A LOVE RISK

Are you ready to take a love risk? Here are five bold ways to release the imprisoned splendor God has *already placed* inside of you:

### 1. COME RIGHT OUT AND SAY IT.

If you want to be inundated with love, become a love waterfall, always pouring it on other people.

LOVE WITHOUT
EXPRESSION IS USELESS.

Some people say, "I'm not wired that way." My father was one of those. He came from a family who thought that if you told people how wonderful they were, it built up their pride, so they rarely expressed approval. He married my mother, who was very expressive, and one day she told him, "You don't express your love, but I'm going to make you a lover." She constantly kissed him and told him how wonderful he was, and by the time I was a little boy he had changed entirely. I never knew him as that cold man he had been. He was warm, loving, engaging and encouraging.

Most men I see for marital counseling say, "She never does this or that for me." That tells me they're still thinking *forward*, not *backward*. Love has to be given before it can ever be received. It's not what your spouse does for you that counts—it's what you do for your spouse.

I bet if you said "I love you" more, it would redefine your relationships. Try it. If you tell people you love them, you will hear it back. How many times have you ended a phone conversation with someone close to you, and said, "I love you," then heard those words come back to you? Doesn't it feel nice to say what your heart feels?

## 2. PUT YOUR LOVE IN WRITING.

I keep an "I love you" file for the nice letters I get. When I feel discouraged, I pull the file out and read them. It's one thing to hear it, but it's another to touch it and see it.

In my "I love you" file is a rock. It came from a young pastor who came to our pastor's school. He went to pray on the side of the mountain by our church, claimed his city for God and took a rock as a reminder. He went home and built a great church and sent me the rock, which was very important to him, as a way of returning the love he felt we had given him.

Now that rock encourages me!

Writing down your love makes it permanent and lasting. It gives people life preservers if they are ever drowning in despair. There's nothing like having love letters stashed away in a desk or closet for use when you really need them.

## 3. DO AN OUTRAGEOUSLY LOVING THING.

One day a businessman in my church took his wife to the nicest restaurant in Phoenix. After dinner he suggested they walk to a nearby luxurious hotel and look around. They walked through and admired the lush gardens and soaring architecture, so he suggested they take a look in one of the rooms, just to see how nice it was. The manager obliged and took them to a room. He opened the door to the room, and it was full of flowers addressed to the businessman's wife! The whole thing had been planned in advance as a surprise romantic getaway.

That's the kind of experience you don't soon forget! It warms your heart for a lifetime.

Another man I know took his wife to eat at the airport, and while they dined he asked her where she would go if she could take a plane anywhere. She said she'd go visit her mother who was ill. He snapped his fingers, and people materialized with her suitcases all packed. He said, "I thought that's what you'd say," and handed her a ticket to go visit her mother.

That's hard to beat! But if you let your imagination dream a bit and think of the wildest thing you could do to show love to your spouse, or even to a good friend, I bet you could come up with something better.

My son Matthew became pastor of the Dream Center at age twenty. He made the same commitment I had made and would not date girls in his church. Five years and one day later he told me he thought he had found the right girl. She had come to America from Sweden to work in the ministry when she was seventeen. She took over the food program at the Dream Center and was a beautiful, dedicated girl. Matthew told me he'd had his eye on her, and he asked my advice about dating her. I said, "Of course you can date her—you've waited long enough."

Three months later, after many meetings with this young lady about the food ministry, he knew he wanted to marry her. So he cooked up a romantic plan to surprise her and propose, all at the same time.

He had discovered that she had a life goal to see the Empire State Building. So he arranged for her to go to New York City at the invitation of Bill Wilson, ostensibly to help Bill's church learn more about doing food ministry. Matthew put her on a plane and said good-bye.

She was to speak the night she arrived, but when she landed the driver said, "We've got some time before the service, and I understand you've wanted to see the Empire State Building." He took her to that famous landmark.

Unknown to her, Matthew had flown in and was already on the observation deck hiding behind the air conditioner, waiting for her. When she appeared, Matthew sneaked up behind her and greeted her. She nearly fainted. Then he turned to the hundreds of people on top of the building and said, "Attention, everybody. I'm getting ready to ask this girl to marry me. I hope she doesn't refuse." He went on to announce to everyone all the qualities that attracted him to her. When he finished all the tourists clapped. "Will you marry me?" he asked her.

All she could say was, "Yes, yes, yes!"

## LET YOUR LOVE BE OUTRAGEOUS FOR A WHILE.

Then there was a second surprise. I had saved up frequent flier miles and was able to fly our whole family to New York. We met Matthew and his soon-to-be bride at a beautiful restaurant on the lake in Central Park. The next day we went shopping, and my daughter and her husband, whom the Lord has blessed financially, took Matthew's fiancée to Saks Fifth Avenue and bought her a wedding dress.

That's the language of love! I bet any woman would love to have such a surprise. Now that they are married, Matthew continues to surprise her. One night he rented a Jaguar, picked her up and took her to a beautiful place on the beach. Another time he took her horseback riding.

Make your life memorable. Make an otherwise ordinary day extraordinary. Let your love be outrageous for a while.

## 4. REJOICE WITH THOSE WHO REJOICE, AND WEEP WITH THOSE WHO WEEP.

Sometimes showing love is about helping someone who's in no mood to celebrate. I know a man, a close friend, who lost his young son. I went through that time of mourning with him, and as a result we are close friends today and can talk about virtually anything. I asked him once if it embarrassed him or made him sad to talk about his son, and he said no. So we often talked about our boys and what his son might have done had he been alive. That was a way of showing love to him in a way he needed.

Sharing grief with someone, or walking through the valley with them, lays deep foundations of love and trust. Jesus went to weddings and to funerals. He knew what people needed in both circumstances. We should be comfortable showing love to the joyful and to the mourning.

## 5. LEARN TO LOVE PEOPLE IN DIFFERENT WAYS.

Just as I had to learn that each of my children receives and gives love differently, so we must learn to love people in different ways.

There have been books and studies about the different "love languages" people speak. It's critical for you to learn how to give and receive love with those close to you. Study your children, pay attention to your spouse, be sensitive to your friends—how do they relate and show companionship or affection? Is it with words, hugs, gifts, special celebrations or just being together? Figure it out, and you'll show love in a way that makes everyone feel great.

## LOVE IS FOREVER

People remember love, not sermons. Twenty years from now when people talk about Tommy Barnett, I'm sure they won't remember any more than one or two of my sermons. But I trust they will remember years of consistent, sincere love that I have tried to show to them.

## IF YOU WANT SOMEONE TO LOVE YOU, START LOVING SOMEONE ELSE.

What is it you remember about a person? Their wit? Their intelligence? In the end, it's only love that matters. Love is what gives us eternal value. Everyone wants to be recognized as spiritual creatures made in the image of God, and love is the only way to do that. Love is the language the heart speaks.

People are like faucets. You can spin around some faucet handles endlessly, but the water never comes out. Some drip a little bit, but never enough to satisfy. Some turn on and off at acceptable times, and their outflow is carefully measured. Some gush when you barely turn them, and others won't turn off even when you try!

That's how love is. If we drip-drip love to others, God drip-drips love to us. If we flow all the time, God takes a fire hose and cranks it on high, keeping our reservoir full.

You are an extremely wealthy person. You have infinite love in you. Remember the outlet found in the forest in our opening paragraphs? Are you plugging in to it, creating ways for that love-power to flow? If you want someone to love you, start loving someone else.

God's only going to give us as much love for others as we will use. Love as if your love is unlimited, and you will find it is. Love is not for a rainy day. Don't store it up. It's a checking account, not a savings account. You may not love someone when you first meet that person, but if you give the love you have, it will grow.

I challenge you to be the *lovingest* person you know, and I can tell you in advance that your supply will never run dry.

# EIGHT

# ENCOURAGEMENT

I sat in the foyer of the college president's office, shaking in my boots and waiting for him to come in. A few days earlier I had told the dean of my decision to leave Bible college after only one year. I was restless and wanting to get out and change the world. The dean had told the president, and the president called me in for a meeting, which I had been dreading with all my heart.

Bible school hadn't suited me the way I thought it would. While I was in high school I held revival services throughout Texas during the summer, and there were many wonderful times with people being saved and filled with the Holy Spirit. After a summer of revival services I went back to high school in the fall.

The summer after I'd graduated from high school, I bought a five-hundred-seat tent and traveled through Kansas and Oklahoma holding revivals. All my friends were going off to Bible school, and I wondered if I was missing out. So I enrolled. But having been raised in a very successful pastor's home, I knew a lot about ministry, and what they gave me to learn seemed elementary. On top of that, my standards while I was an evangelist were stricter than when I was a student. As an evangelist I never dated and never went out on the town. But in Bible college I had no such limits. I dated girls and went to the big city with my friends and had a ball.

But I wasn't learning anything, and I came under conviction about my actions. I told my parents that I felt I needed to be out preaching, and they suggested I go on the evangelistic field and take Bible courses by correspondence. I liked that advice and made the decision to stop attending Bible college.

And that's why I had landed in the president's office, awaiting a meeting with the most intimidating man on campus.

His office was like an inner sanctum, a holy of holies—or, at this moment, a torture chamber. It was classical in its design and lined with theological books. Then the president came in, a bear of a man who towered over my one-hundred-twenty-five-pound frame.

He welcomed me, sat down, leaned on his desk and looked me in the eye.

"I understand you want to leave Bible college," he said, and let the silence hang for a moment.

"Yes, sir, I do," I said. As politely as I could, I explained my reasons, and he listened thoughtfully. I told him I felt that much of what I was learning was repetitious. I explained my background as I grew up in my father's house and concluded that I should be about my calling as an evangelist.

"That might be true," he said, "but once the other students graduate from Bible college they will soon pass you by. Why not stick with it and get your education? It will help you in the long run."

I thanked him for his advice, but my mind was made up.

He considered my words for another moment and was quiet for a while. Then he said words I would never forget.

"If you quit Bible school, you'll fail," he said. "You'll go out and pastor a church somewhere, but you'll never do anything significant. You'll be a one-horse preacher and have a little work in some city. By most standards you'll do all right, but you'll only get so far. You'll have put a limit on your ministry."

I couldn't say anything in response because of the lump in my throat, but I also felt a hard knot of resolve in my stomach. I knew I wouldn't turn back. He stood up, I stood up, we shook hands, and I left his office.

I left with an almost crushing feeling of discouragement, but I knew I was doing the will of God. I decided I would do everything I could to get an education by studying, reading widely, traveling and associating with great people—but I wouldn't let the president's words be true.

That conversation rang in my ears for years,

even to this day. Why? Because it was a challenge. I wanted to prove him wrong, and not just him, but also anyone who doubted God's visions in my heart.

Fortunately, my parents were the most positive people in the world. My dad counter-balanced any negative influence with his simple, straightforward, "You can do it." That encouragement meant the world to me.

That day in the president's office, I didn't know whether I would succeed or not, but I was determined to try. And I made up my mind that I was going to be an encourager. I would never use my words to kill a man's dream, no matter how crazy I thought that man was.

## BEING DREAM-BUILDERS

Words can bind men up or set them free. Words can knock you off track or set you back on track. The world is full of cynics, discouragers and dream-killers. Turn on the television, and you see them talking. Open a newspaper, and you see the litany of bad news and dire predictions.

If we're already giving away our time, money and love, shouldn't we also give away encouragement? Christians ought to be people of encouragement. After all, it was Jesus who said:

> Do not be afraid, little flock, for your Father
> has been pleased to give you the kingdom.
> —LUKE 12:32

Encouraging people is the right thing to do, and it also has a benefit for us. Let me ask you this: Have you ever wanted to encourage someone who discouraged you? Usually not. You want to encourage someone in return for encouraging you. That's how this principle works.

You get encouragement by being an encourager. You sow encouragement by telling other people to follow their dreams, by getting on board with them when they share their crazy ideas. One day that encouragement you sow will come back to you as a full harvest.

In my own church I brag on people instead of berating them. Some pastors vent their frustration at people who do not want to do ministry, bring in the homeless or feed the hungry. I go the other way. On Sunday morning I tell my people, "Lots of churches won't bring in ragamuffin kids or spend so much money to reach people, but I'm glad this church isn't like that." I give positive affirmation, and people live up to it. I encourage them in the right direction instead of discouraging them by scolding them.

> YOU GET ENCOURAGEMENT
> BY BEING AN ENCOURAGER.

Throughout history, dream-killers have tried to shout down dreamers. Edwin Drake, the first man to drill for oil in the United States (back in 1859), heard these words from onlookers: "Drill for oil? You mean drill into the ground to try and find oil? You're crazy."

When in 1865 the *Boston Post* heard that some inventors were working on a device to allow voices to be transmitted across great distances using wires, it wrote, "Well-informed people know it is impossible to transmit the voice over wires, and that were it possible to do so, the thing would be of no practical value." Think of what Alexander Graham Bell must have thought when he read that!

Charles Duell, director of the U.S. Patent Office in 1899, said, "Everything that can be invented has been invented." That was before even the automobile.

Lord Kelvin, one of the nineteenth century's top experts on thermodynamics, said in the 1890s, "Heavier-than-air flying machines are impossible." Of course, the Wright brothers proved him wrong.

The *New York Times* in 1936 said that "a rocket will never be able to leave the earth's atmosphere."

THE WORLD DOESN'T
NEED ANOTHER DREAM-
KILLER. I TRY HARD TO BE AN
ENCOURAGER, A DREAM-BUILDER.

Darryl Zanuck, producer from Twentieth-Century Fox, said in 1946, "Television won't last because people will soon get tired of staring at a plywood box every night."

And Elvis Presley was told by a successful performer at the Grand Ole Opry, "You ain't going nowhere, son. You ought to go back to driving a truck."[1]

The mistake, of course, is to listen to the dream-killers. That's why encouragement is so important. It holds open the possibility that the future may be more exciting, more mind-boggling than we think. It refuses to say no to an idea, even if it seems foolish. Perhaps that crazy idea is just ahead of its time!

There is no such thing as an impossible dream. I wonder how many people will one day discover that they spent their lives killing other people's dreams. I picture certain people, like weed-control experts, walking around a lawn and spraying weed poison on every flower that tries to pop up. Their words are really dream-poison. They ridicule and mock ideas God has planted. I shudder to think what God will say to them on Judgment Day.

One thing is for sure—the world doesn't need another dream-killer. I try hard to be an encourager, a dream-builder. Even if I'm skeptical, I try to hold my tongue!

I remember meeting Larry Kerychuk, a former professional football player in the Canadian Football League (CFL) who was injured and couldn't play anymore. During my first week in Phoenix, he sat in my house—with no furniture, nothing—until 3 A.M. and told me he had a dream to hold a Spirit-filled conference for athletes. He wanted to have a training site for world-class athletes to train for the Olympics and go through a discipleship program at the same time.

I thought, *This guy's a big dreamer, but he can't pull that off.*

But I said, "Praise God. Go for it."

He did! He started the conference, and today the best athletes in the world come to train. Barry Sanders was filled with the Holy Spirit while he was there. So was Bill McCartney. Dozens of other professional athletes have attended throughout the years.

But that's not all. Two years ago Larry was given the Phoenix Swim Club, worth five million dollars. He used it as a training facility for Olympic athletes, and at the Olympics in Australia we qualified eleven people and won four gold medals, two silver and two bronze.

I encouraged Larry even when I didn't believe him, and he encouraged the athletes—and look at the results!

## NO HOPELESS PEOPLE

Discouragement is like having spiritual AIDS. It suppresses your immune system, makes you vulnerable to sickness and causes you to waste away physically and spiritually. Surgeons don't like to operate on discouraged people because it's as if their body can't fight back.

Encouraging people is like giving them a cure for their disease. It's like going on a rescue mission or throwing out a life preserver. When people are discouraged, they make bad choices and can easily ruin their lives. Encouragement literally saves people from an early grave.

There's a young man named Aaron Jayne who came to one of our pageants in Phoenix where we had a laser light show. He had no interest in the gospel, but he had heard that if you loaded up on drugs, the laser lights would look incredible. He was high when he came to the service. But he ended up getting saved. Not long after that he told me that his doctor and former pastor had told him he was a hopeless drug addict and would never make it.

Those were the words of a dream-killer.

I took Aaron by the shoulder and told him I had hope for him. "Report to me next Sunday night so I know that you've gone a week without drugs," I said.

He reported to me the next Sunday to say he had gone without drugs, so I had him report to me the following week, and so on. Then I said to report to me in a month. Then he made it a year, and two years. By that time he had proven the doctor's words false and had become a priceless member of our congregation.

> ENCOURAGING PEOPLE
> IS LIKE GIVING THEM A
> CURE FOR THEIR DISEASE.

When we started the Dream Center, Aaron came as a volunteer. It wasn't long before he became the youth leader. Seven years later Aaron is our evangelist and preaches all over the world. He's building Dream Centers all over Europe. All it took to rescue him from hopelessness were a few words of encouragement at a crucial time in his life. Now he shares encouragement with countless thousands.

Earlier I mentioned José, our Spanish pastor,

who gave his testimony when George W. Bush visited the Dream Center. When José was released from prison he was trying to set a pattern for a better life, so he came as a volunteer. We did nothing but encourage him. That encouragement was like sunlight and water to him, and he has grown into a terrific pastor and an indispensable part of our team. He pastors two services every Sunday morning for our Spanish-speaking church.

Rick Seward, a friend of mine, is one of the great pastors in Singapore. A number of years ago he was discouraged because of the opposition he was facing from the government, so he and his wife came to Phoenix to clear their heads and get some rest. I rented an apartment for them for a month so they could be refreshed, and we sent him home with a big offering. The Sewards went home with renewed vision, and later when I was in one of my lowest hours, wondering how we were going to raise enough money to meet a strict deadline and keep the Dream Center open, their church gave us one of our largest gifts. Their gift helped to keep the Dream Center open. The money was sorely needed, but the encouragement Rick gave me at that time was invaluable.

Jack Wallace, one of my pastors, became addicted to the pain pills he was prescribed as the result of repeated surgeries. I released him for a year and sent him to rehabilitation. As he put his life back together, I kept encouraging him to keep his eyes on the prize. After his rehabilitation he took a church of four hundred in Detroit. Now, eight years later, his ministry averages over six thousand in attendance. They recently gave half a million dollars to the Dream Center as a way of sowing back into the people who encouraged him.

## REAL REVIVAL?

When I was in South Africa, I toured one of the cities with a pastor. As we toured, we came upon a Charismatic church that had been closed down. Homeless people descended upon this church for some unknown reason. They built their shanties around the church, but the people of the church ignored them. The government told the homeless people to move—the neighbors didn't want them and the community was up in arms. Day after day the story made front-page news in the newspaper, but the homeless would not move. Finally they were threatened with jail.

In the middle of the night, the pastor received a call from a policeman who belonged to his congregation informing him that the homeless people would be jailed in the morning. The pastor sent trucks to gather them up and took them to a piece of property the church owned. Eventually the church built houses for them.

Here's the irony of that situation: The Charismatic church that had ignored the homeless people was experiencing what they called a *Holy Ghost revival.* There was great singing, and people were slain in the Spirit, speaking in tongues, laughing and dancing. To get inside the sanctuary, the people had to step over the homeless people who had camped around their church. But taking care of the homeless apparently wasn't part of their theology.

A newspaper reporter visited the homeless people and asked if anyone from the church had offered them help or encouragement. The people said no one had.

I contend that that church wouldn't know what revival was if it hit them in the face. Today the church has actually closed down. They had the workings of revival right around them, but they refused to encourage.

## IT COMES BACK TO YOU

Encouragement is like everything else we have been discussing. When you give it, it comes back in greater measure. I get nearly all my encouragement from people I encouraged at one time. It's like putting money in a mutual fund and remembering later, during a time when you really need it, that the money is there, and then discovering that it has gained significant interest.

You can invest encouragement in people, and someday when you need to make a withdrawal, you'll receive more than you gave because God will add His blessing to it.

And if nobody else encourages you, God will! When Paul was in jail with no one to buck him up, Jesus came to encourage him! God saw all the letters Paul was writing to encourage the churches he'd planted, so when Paul was left alone, God personally breathed new life into Paul's dreams.

My son Matthew is the most encouraging person I know. Every week on Thursday night he has a guest preacher at the Dream Center, and he makes them feel so wonderful that they feel like Billy Graham, Oral Roberts and Mother Teresa all in one. Matthew tells every guest that his or her sermon is the most awesome sermon he's ever heard, and he means it!

> WHEN YOU GIVE
> ENCOURAGEMENT, IT COMES
> BACK IN GREATER MEASURE.

People don't believe me when I say I don't enjoy preaching, but I do enjoy watching others preach. I would rather see other people succeed than succeed myself. I get more joy out of their success than mine. That's why we have two hundred ministries in Phoenix and almost two hundred at the Dream Center. Some pastors won't allow ministries to grow within their church because they're threatened. They think another man will be raised up and branch off into another church. I feel the opposite. I want people to be raised up. I encourage them to do something bigger than what I'm doing.

## HEALTHY COMPETITION

I used to play golf with my son Luke, and I'd beat him by seventy-five strokes. But I encouraged him the whole way. "Someday you'll beat me," I'd say.

"No, I won't," he'd respond dejectedly.

Then the day came when I could only beat him by fifty strokes, and I told him once again that soon he'd beat me. He still didn't believe it, but we both knew he was getting better.

Then came the day when he was only twenty strokes behind. Just about that time I began to tell him the opposite: "You'll never catch up with me," I told him. That fired his determination even more.

Then he came within ten strokes.

Then five.

Finally the day came when he beat me. Now I can't beat him. The encouragement I gave him paid off, along with the effort he put into it. Now he turns the tables on me and says, "Come on, Dad. Keep practicing, and someday you'll golf as well as I do!"

Not everyone you encourage will succeed, but some will. Some will fail, then give up. Some will fail at first, and then go on to greatness.

Masaru Ibuka and Akio Morita had both failed in some way before they partnered in business together. Ibuka failed his exam for lifetime employment at Toshiba, but he didn't give up. He and Morita made an automatic rice cooker, but the machine burned rice, and they only sold a hundred of them.

Then they teamed up to build an inexpensive tape recorder, which they sold to Japanese schools. That was the beginning of the Sony Corporation.

Henry Ford's first business, the Detroit

Automobile Company, failed within two years
due to partnership disputes. Ford's second
automobile company also failed. Only on his
third try did he succeed with the Ford Motor
Company.

Phillip Knight wanted to build a shoe company, but ran into problems. His manufacturer
wanted majority ownership of his company.
Knight refused and was left without a product to
sell. He had an idea for a waffle-sole shoe design
and began selling them on his own until a dock
workers' strike and fluctuations in Japanese cur-
rency almost put him out of business. His
company barely survived. But survive it did—
and today it is known around the world: Nike.

Most everyone loves the gourmet pizzas at
California Pizza Kitchen, but it too was started
by "failures." Rick Rosenfield and Larry Flax co-
wrote a screenplay they couldn't sell, started an
Italian restaurant that went bankrupt and
launched a mobile skateboard park that failed. It
wasn't until they started selling pizzas that success clicked for them.[2]

When I hear stories like that I am encouraged
to keep going despite setbacks.

## WARTS AND ALL

Sometimes people don't understand that pastors
need encouragement. When I feel beaten down
by life, when all my energies are tapped out and
discouragement looms, one scripture sustains me
more than any other:

Elijah was a man just like us.

—JAMES 5:17

Or, as another translation puts it, Elijah "was a man subject to like passions as we are" (KJV).

All I have to do is read that, and my spirits are lifted. I'm so glad God put men's faults and warts in the Bible to remind us that we don't need to be perfect. Elijah was a great man, but he was not so great that he didn't get discouraged now and then—just as I do.

I have been privileged to know some of the great men of this century, men who to others are only hallowed names in history books. These men include William Branham, Jack Coe, Ernest Williams, Oral Roberts, T. D. Jakes, David Yonggi Cho and Robert Schuller. Men whose names will one day be enshrined as the greats of our generation are men I have known personally.

I'M SO GLAD GOD PUT
MEN'S FAULTS AND WARTS IN
THE BIBLE TO REMIND US THAT
WE DON'T NEED TO BE PERFECT.

One time I was asked if I was encouraged by the strength I saw in these men, and I instinctively said that no, I was not encouraged by their strength but by their weakness. It was their humanity that impressed me. They were the best of men—but still men at best. They had doubts, fears, tears, failures and sins. This awareness of their imperfections encourages me more than anything else when I think about them.

I think of John Mark, the first pastor of the church at Alexandria. He wrote the Gospel of Mark and eventually died a martyr's death. But before that he went with Paul and Barnabas to Pamphylia, a wild place infested with snakes and dangerous animals. John Mark left that journey and went home, perhaps because he was scared or discouraged or tired or hungry. His abandonment upset Paul so much that Paul wouldn't take John Mark with him on subsequent journeys.

John Mark—a great man, author of one of the four Gospels, a Christian martyr—yet he wanted to quit and go home.

*Just as I do sometimes.*

There was no greater man ever born than John the Baptist, yet he doubted his own salvation and wondered if Jesus was the Messiah. His discouragement was that strong.

*Just as mine is sometimes.*

Wesley and Whitfield, two of the greatest Christians in history, couldn't get along and wouldn't speak to each other.

For a period of time, John Calvin and Martin Luther wouldn't sit in the same room with each other.

D. L. Moody had such a hot temper that one night when a man came to the altar cursing him, Moody punched him out.

The great Charles Spurgeon smoked cigars.

All these men had foibles and flaws. And that's what tells me they were just like me.

I remember golfing with one of America's great pastors when I was a young man. He was very competitive, and when I hit a ball close to a tree I asked if I could move the ball. "No way," he said. But later when he hit a ball close to a tree he moved it. I pointed this out, and he said, "Your tree was planted by the Indians, so you can't move it. But this tree was planted by the golf course, so I can move mine." He was just as shifty as I am!

I remember a time when my dad went to pastor a church in Texas. He did it against God's will, and it was a time of unbroken misery for two years for him and the rest of us. He was as close to getting away from God as he ever got because of his discouragement. It hurt his marriage and put us all in a funk until Dad got back on the right track. But strangely enough, those memories encourage me, because I saw the man I idolized going through the valley and realized he was a man like me. If he could make it through, so could I in my times of misery.

One time at a conference I heard Kenneth Copeland talk about an extended fast he had undertaken. At one point during the fast he asked God to kill him because he'd gone through such depression and discouragement. That encouraged me more than any victory rally I've ever been to!

I spend my life trying to encourage other pastors, but I do it by telling them how discouraged I get! Every Monday morning I say I'm going to quit pastoring, but first I'll have a cup of coffee. Starbucks has saved my ministry more than any person! On bad mornings I have two cups, and I say, "Lord, I'll go another week." When I tell pastors that, they perk up and realize I'm like them.

I tell them about the time I was preaching that God was still on the throne when I bent over and ripped open the seat of my pants. I quickly wrapped up that sermon, backed off the platform and ran to my car.

### ENCOURAGEMENT IS MORE POTENT THAN ANY DRUG ON THE MARKET.

There's nothing more encouraging than the failure of a man you admire. But it's good to remember that the failure didn't make them great—their ability to overcome it, with God's help, is what made them great.

Encouragement is more potent than any drug on the market. It imparts something no chemical company can: real, genuine hope. I encourage you once and for all to choose to be an encourager, a dream-builder, a cheerleader for people. The words cost nothing for you to give, but they will prove priceless to those who receive them.

# NINE

# IDEAS

Have you ever had a really good idea that you thought would bless the world?

Maybe it was for a ministry or a play or a song. Maybe it was an idea for a business or product or service.

Sometimes people talk to me about their ideas. If they ask for advice on how to carry it out, I tell them the same thing: *Give that idea away.*

Do I mean give the idea to someone else and let that person accomplish it and reap the benefits? Not necessarily. Sometimes giving away an idea means sharing it with others and gaining support for it. Sometimes it does mean letting someone else run with it, if they're better equipped to make it a success.

But it always means having a giving attitude about the ideas God places in our hearts.

## RAW MATERIAL FOR SUCCESS

Giving ideas is like taking our encouragement one step further. Encouragement gives people the faith to try. Ideas give them the tools to carry it out.

Some of the world's great businesses were built on borrowed ideas. For example, it wasn't the McDonald brothers who made the golden arches a staple of the American landscape—it was Ray Kroc, a failed Florida real estate salesman. He met the brothers while selling milk shake machines. At the time they had one restaurant in San Bernardino, California, where they served low-priced hamburgers. But it was Kroc who had the vision to franchise McDonald's. He later bought them out and built it into the largest food-service company in the world, with more than twenty thousand restaurants. When you go into a McDonald's restaurant today, the plaque you often see near the counter memorializes not the McDonald brothers who had the idea, but Kroc, who made the idea great.[1]

And it wasn't Cliff's idea to help students by synopsizing great books in small pamphlets called *CliffsNotes*—it was Jack Cole, a Canadian bookstore owner. Over dinner, Cole shared the idea with Clifton Hillegass, then a bookseller from Nebraska. Cole had published condensations of sixteen Shakespeare plays and called them *Cole's Notes*. Hillegass liked the idea and partnered with Cole to distribute them, changing the name to *CliffsNotes* and giving them bright yellow and black covers.

By the end of that year, 1958, Hillegass had sold fifty-eight thousand, and by the time Hillegass sold the business many years later, *CliffsNotes* was selling more than five million pamphlets a year and had grown to include every major work studied by high school and college students.[2]

> ENCOURAGEMENT
> GIVES PEOPLE
> THE FAITH TO TRY.
> IDEAS GIVE THEM THE
> TOOLS TO CARRY IT OUT.

It wasn't Cliff Hillegass' idea, but he made it great.

Many businesses are built on borrowed ideas. What if the men we just talked about hadn't shared their ideas? What if they refused to let someone run with it? The world would be a poorer place.

## IDEA SHARING

I have spent my life giving ideas away. Some people ask me why I do it. It's because I value ideas more than credit and because it brings glory and honor to God and to others. Do not despise your own thoughts or ideas—you may be despising the thoughts of God because God speaks through thoughts and ideas.

Everywhere I go I find that churches are running buses, having Fourth of July celebrations, using illustrated sermons and even holding pastor's conferences.

There are Dream Centers everywhere since Matthew and I started the Los Angeles Dream Center in 1994. Joyce Meyer has one in St. Louis. Billy Joe Daugherty has one in Tulsa. There are nearly two hundred in all. In a way, having all the other Dream Centers out there has hurt the original Dream Center because people in those cities who used to support us are now supporting their local versions.

But I'd rather spread around a good idea than keep it to myself. And I know that when I give ideas, I get more ideas in return.

Here is why this principle works:

IDEAS CREATE MORE IDEAS.

Most of us have sat in on brainstorming sessions where you go around the table and everybody tosses out their best ideas for consideration. Usually there are two or three really good ideas that go on to become realities, and the very best ideas seem to be those that are sparked by what someone else says. Their idea strikes your mind in a certain way and creates a synergy that leads to a new, better idea. It is my guess that ten people sharing ideas in one room would generate better results than ten people in ten isolated rooms trying to do it alone.

Ideas are the seedbed for more ideas. Only by planting ideas can you reap better ones. When I share ideas, I know someone else will add his or her own idea to it, and the end result will be better than what I began with. That's why I'm willing to share. I'd rather share credit for a world-changing idea than have sole credit for a so-so idea.

WHEN YOU SHARE YOUR IDEAS, OTHER PEOPLE SHARE THEIR GOOD IDEAS WITH YOU.

I remember as a kid how important it was to take credit for things. Kids often say, "It was my idea! I thought of it first!"

Thankfully, that attitude wears off (in most people) as they become adults. We learn how to share openly and not worry about who gets the credit.

And when we don't care about credit, the spirit of generosity prevails. More Dream Centers sprouting up in other cities have blessed us back as those centers share their techniques and strategies for ministry. We gave them the initial idea, and now they share their ideas and discoveries with us.

> I'D RATHER SPREAD
> AROUND A GOOD IDEA
> THAN KEEP IT TO MYSELF.

Through the years I've written and performed illustrated sermons, many of which I've printed and given away. Now I get great ideas for illustrated sermons from pastors and writers who send me their scripts. I hardly have to think of my own anymore!

I'm giving all my ideas to my boys because my dad gave his ideas to me. He was a great promoter. He taught me how to give an altar call and do bus ministry, and I have passed that, and more, on to my boys. For instance, our Phoenix church has an Easter pageant every year. One year, Luke called and said he was doing an Easter trilogy instead of a pageant. For three Sundays in a row he was having illustrated sermons about the life, death and resurrection of Jesus. I borrowed that good idea, and now that's what I do for Easter. This idea has become the number one thing that helps us grow every year. In fact, many of my sermon ideas now come from my sons.

## WHEN YOU HOARD IDEAS, YOU STOP THE FLOW.

Matthew had an idea for reaching nearby neighborhoods in Los Angeles, so he started Adopt-a-Block. I thought it was a terrific idea, and we have implemented it in Phoenix. Now our church is experiencing the greatest revival I've ever seen because Matthew shared his idea with me.

My daughter and her husband are two of the biggest givers in our church, but I remember when he was first starting his business. Today his business has grown, and their giving makes many ideas possible.

## WHEN YOU GIVE AWAY IDEAS, GOD GIVES YOU MORE IDEAS.

This is the same principle we've discussed throughout this book. The only way to keep having ideas is by giving ideas away as quickly as you get them. I believe God rewards generosity in the realm of ideas just as He does with time, money, energy, love and encouragement.

Remember, we don't own ideas—God does. And when you hoard ideas, you stop the flow. As we've seen, nothing in life can be kept by hoarding. Jesus gave His best ideas away. He said:

> ...for everything that I learned from my Father I have made known to you.
> —JOHN 15:15

He didn't need to be "da man" by holding on to what the Father gave Him. He understood that hoarding wasn't the way to minister effectively.

Prime the pump of your creativity by giving away ideas. God will pay you back richly.

WHEN YOU GIVE AWAY IDEAS, GOD EMPOWERS THE IDEAS YOU HAVE.

Have you known people who get a great idea for a business or ministry, then spend much of their energy keeping it a secret so they can develop it and reap all the benefits? Those ideas tend to die because they are surrounded by a spirit of jealousy.

But when we develop our ideas with a spirit of generosity, God breathes life into them.

A good idea is no guarantee of success. In fact, good ideas are a dime a dozen. It's the follow-through that counts. There has to be hard work and a coming together of people who believe in the idea. God has to supply the resources to make it happen. When you are generous and willing to share credit, the favor of God will rest upon you and all you put your hand to. Your idea will be empowered to become reality.

## From Idea to Reality

One of the first ways to make an idea a reality is to speak it. Put it in the airwaves, and plant it in other people's minds; let the world know you have a great idea and are looking for ways to carry it out.

PRIME THE PUMP
OF YOUR CREATIVITY BY
GIVING AWAY IDEAS. GOD
WILL PAY YOU BACK RICHLY.

One day I stood in the pulpit and told my church we were going to build a retirement home. In all honesty, I didn't want to build a retirement home. We'd done so much else that I was tired of getting people excited about big projects. I didn't want to spend time on it or raise money for it, but I felt it was a need that God would bless.

Someone who owns a winter home in Phoenix and is in the business of building retirement homes heard me that morning. The idea caught in his mind and motivated him. He got in contact with me and offered to buy a parcel of property right next door to the church and build a retirement home—all without my having to lift a finger. So our retirement home was built next door because a businessman heard a God-inspired idea and caught the vision.

When you speak the word you become a channel that releases that idea into reality. The ideas are God's, but the responsibility to speak them is ours.

Before I had any idea how it could happen, I started talking about having an AIDS hospice at the Dream Center. I envisioned it, described it, pictured it and told people about it until they started asking me how it was going to happen. Then members of our team took it upon themselves and found ways to make it happen. People sought solutions when I put the idea into the airwaves.

One time I stood in the pulpit and said that someday we would have a medical trailer. A banker heard that and gave the first $50,000 toward it.

The same is true of our unwed mothers' home and most other ministries in our church. They started as ideas and grew because we talked about them, and then got to work.

I used to say from the pulpit, "Someday, somebody is going to give me a million dollars." It was around the time when people gave Jerry Falwell and Robert Schuller each a million dollars, so I'd say, "God loves me as much or more than them." Then one day a man gave me a million. The next week his son gave a million. In the last four years nine people have given me a million dollars.

I've decided to start talking about one *billion*

dollars. Why not? If it's God's idea, it will happen.

Ideas are valuable things, but they really work only when we share them, give them away and let other people share the credit. After all, "there is nothing new under the sun" (Eccles. 1:9). Any good idea we get comes not from our brilliance but from the generosity of God.

# TEN

# FORGIVENESS

Jim Bakker is a dear friend of mine, a wonderful man and a humble believer. He has been through more trials than most people. His successes and failures have played out in public, and his life hasn't gone the way he would have planned. But today he is a living example that God doesn't give up on us.

I first met Jim a long time ago when he was hosting the *PTL Club.* He would have me on, and we got along well because soulwinning was the top priority for both of us. Many years later, in 1994, he was released from prison. At that time, Jim told me that few people wanted to associate with him.

Jim came to our pastor's school to hear his son give his testimony. It was the first time he had been in a church since getting out of prison. Then in 1995, Jim was in Los Angeles, and I invited him to speak at the Dream Center's Thursday night service. At the time he was very much a hurting man. Years of prison life had drummed into him that he was worthless. He felt totally alienated from the church at large because he thought he was a disgrace, an embarrassment.

He walked into our gymnasium that night broken, in his own words, like a whipped puppy, fearful of what people would think about or say to him.

But when he stepped into the pulpit, something amazing happened. Part way through his message Jim stopped and asked if anyone else in the room had been in prison; more than half of the people raised their hands. Jim said, partly in jest, "I finally found my people!" Later he told me that at that moment he realized he was more of a prisoner than a preacher because of the great impact prison had had on his mind.

Jim was so moved that night that he asked to stay a few more days, not in a nearby hotel but at the Dream Center, so we gave him a room like everybody else. After a week of sitting in on every ministry we had, Jim asked me if he could live there. He had been impressed by Matthew, who went visiting men and women ravaged by sin and wasn't afraid to hug them though they smelled strongly of urine. He'd been bowled over by the Adopt-a-Block and sidewalk Sunday school programs.

And he was overwhelmed by the acceptance he felt. The Spanish children would crowd around him, saying, "Jim Bakker, we love you. Stay here. Live with us." For the first time in years, somebody wanted him around.

Jim timidly asked if I would consider the possibility of him living at the Dream Center as it was the only place he felt accepted, but he warned me that if he lived there it might bring a torrent of negative media coverage. But if the Dream Center was all about restoration, how could we not welcome him? This man was my friend, and God's grace was more important than whatever media coverage his living at the Dream Center would generate, so Matthew and I invited Jim to live at the Dream Center. By God's grace, none of the fears I had of media encampments materialized. There was coverage, but it was positive because the reporters saw Jim's servant heart. It was as if the secular world had gotten past the scandals of the 1980s and didn't want to hear about them anymore, so Jim was left in peace.

He came—a hurting man. But to his wonderful surprise, the inner-city people were eager to love and forgive him. Every day he kept a simple schedule—working, laboring and helping wherever he was needed. He painted the gym beige, installed drapes and help plan our Cinco de Mayo event. Then he began teaching a noontime Bible study in an old laundry room, and it was usually packed to capacity.

Reporters did find him, but they were more subdued this time. They knew Jim had turned down at least one offer from a major television company to host a late-night television show just so he could live at the Dream Center.

"Why?" they wanted to know, and he told them that a miracle was taking place in his life. As he poured his life into other people, God was healing him. Nothing could compare with the grace and forgiveness he felt from the people at the Dream Center.

One day he told me that the only place he went where he felt forgiven by others was at the Dream Center. Why? Because inner-city people know what it's like to have family problems, to make mistakes or to have a brother or relative in jail. They've been down that road before, and they know that only forgiveness can get someone back on their feet.

WITHOUT FORGIVENESS,
YOU MISS THE WHOLE
POINT OF THE GOSPEL.
_____

An amazing thing happened to Jim over the next few years. He regained credibility, not just with believers but also with nonbelievers. I've seen him on *Larry King Live* and other talk shows, and the hosts treat him with noticeable respect. I think they feel safe around Jim because they know he fell about as low as any man could fall, and as a result his heart is tender. He is not judgmental. Everyone watched him go through a type of hell. They saw the title of his book—*I Was Wrong*—which reflected the attitude of his heart, and they realized he had learned from his experiences.

Jim had a potentially more effective ministry

to nonbelievers than ever before. Today he and his beautiful wife, Lori—whom he met at the Los Angeles Dream Center—have their own Dream Center in Panama City, Florida. They are reproducing the forgiveness they received in the most unlikely place—the inner city of Los Angeles!

Isn't everybody looking for forgiveness? Isn't that why people responded so passionately to Jesus—because He didn't condemn them, but freely gave mercy? Every human who has lived long enough knows he or she is a sinner. No one needs that condemnation drilled into him or her continually by others.

What people need is forgiveness.

## GIVING FORGIVENESS

We can give away all the other things we've talked about—time, money, love, energy, encouragement, ideas—but the true sign of a Christian is that he or she readily gives forgiveness. It's essential to the gospel message. Without forgiveness, you miss the whole point of the gospel.

And, like the other things we give, giving forgiveness brings a host of blessings that can literally make the difference between life and death for us.

### WHEN WE FORGIVE, WE RECEIVE FORGIVENESS FROM OTHERS.

It's so simple that we often miss it. Have you ever been around a hard-nosed person who doesn't cut anybody slack? When an unforgiving person makes a mistake, people are less inclined to let him off the hook. He may get forgiven, but it's never that overflowing, abundant forgiveness that comes to people who show that kind of mercy to others.

When you won't forgive someone you are saying you want that person to experience the full punishment for his or her sin. But unforgiveness is a boomerang that comes back stronger and hits you. The forgiveness you give will come back "pressed down, shaken together and running over" (Luke 6:38).

A friend of mine who pastors a large church in another country visited the Dream Center and cried his eyes out at what he saw. On his way home he thought, *I hope someday I have a Dream Center.* When he got home a woman told him someone had given her a large sum of money and some high-rise buildings, which she gave to him. He started his own Dream Center then and there.

I visited his church some time later and toured these buildings, which housed ministries like ours. In one building I saw little boys and girls who had no place to go because their parents had died of AIDS. They were being cared for by my friend's Dream Center.

Then he took me to a building where people were dying of AIDS. I was so moved by the sight of these rail-thin people lying in beds, many of them with church volunteers next to them grasping their hands, stroking their heads and telling them they loved them.

He pointed out a young mother with twin six-year-old girls who came and hugged me. My friend whispered in my ear that they had the AIDS virus. Now it was my turn to want to borrow an idea. On the way home I realized I needed to have that kind of ministry at the Dream Center.

The Los Angeles Dream Center is in an area with lots of homosexuals and drugs—which means AIDS. The Lord spoke to me to gut one floor and make it the most beautiful on the whole campus, and then fill it with people dying of AIDS. The Hyatt Hotel donated furniture, and after lots of hard work, our AIDS hospice was born. It's full of people who will die unless God heals them. Most of them are, or were, homosexuals, and most, if not all of them, get saved.

> BE A PERSON OF MERCY, AND YOU
> WILL WITNESS THE SOFTENING
> OF PEOPLE AROUND YOU—
> EVEN THOSE WHO SEEM SO HARD.

But of all the ministries we have, we don't advertise this one because people won't give to support the AIDS hospice. They think the gays are getting what they deserve. That may be true. But we're giving them forgiveness in the last hours of their lives because I'm keenly aware that if I got what I deserved from God, I'd be in trouble, too.

The hospice is opening up a whole new group to the gospel. Recently the local gay and lesbian center called up and said, "We don't believe like you do, but you've done more for our people than we have. Can you send buses to pick people up from our center and take them to church on Sunday?" As a result, people from that community are getting saved.

Forgiveness works. It gives the gospel its attractiveness. Be a person of mercy, and you will witness the softening of people around you— even those who seem so hard.

WHEN WE FORGIVE, WE MORE READILY FORGIVE OURSELVES.

There was once a handsome, teenage boy, the son of missionaries, who lived on a college campus. Like any young person he had goals and dreams, but he was also a perfectionist and held himself to very high standards. He was devastated anytime he failed, and he drove himself to live an absolutely perfect life.

One night a horrifying discovery was made. The boy was found in his room, stabbed to death. Blood was all over the place. Twelve of the wounds would have been fatal had they been the only ones inflicted. The investigator taped the dormitory off as a crime scene, but then the campus pastor arrived, looked over the scene and said he believed it was a suicide.

"How could it be suicide?" the investigator scoffed. "How could a young man thrust the knife into his head, then keep stabbing himself as he did? Surely it was a murder." The pastor left, but the investigator wondered at his words.

A few days later the coroner's report came back: There was no doubt—it was suicide. Stunned, the investigator visited the pastor at his home and asked how he had known. The pastor said, "A crime like that had to be committed by someone who thoroughly loathed that boy. And no one can hate you as much as you hate yourself."

It was the first suicide on that campus, and it came as the result of a boy who didn't know how to forgive himself.

When we fail to forgive ourselves, we put on the shackles of perfectionism—one of the most damnable bondages I know. No one will make himself holy or perfect by putting his shoulder to the wheel and nose to the grindstone. All of us need to learn to forgive ourselves because all of us will fail.

I've known legalistic people who think that if they get sick they are in sin somehow. I've known others who gave themselves ulcers by trying always to do the right thing.

WHEN WE FAIL TO FORGIVE OURSELVES, WE PUT ON THE SHACKLES OF PERFECTIONISM— ONE OF THE MOST DAMNABLE BONDAGES I KNOW.

If we fail to forgive ourselves, we will shorten our lives, make other people miserable and distance ourselves from the true message of the gospel. You must give yourself permission to fail now and then. Get proficient at forgiving yourself, and you will notice a fresh breeze of grace blowing through your life. You will be more aware of God's goodness, and your heart will become more tender.

## WHEN WE FORGIVE, WE RECEIVE FORGIVENESS FROM GOD.

It's terrifying, but true: God has set up His kingdom so that the only way to receive forgiveness from God is to give it to others. Jesus affirmed this in a story that most of us probably wish He hadn't told. It was about a man who received forgiveness, but failed to give it.

> Then Peter came to Jesus and asked, "Lord, how many times shall I forgive my brother when he sins against me? Up to seven times?"
>
> Jesus answered, "I tell you, not seven times, but seventy-seven times.
>
> "Therefore, the kingdom of heaven is like a king who wanted to settle accounts with his servants. As he began the settlement, a man who owed him ten thousand talents was brought to him. Since he was not able to pay, the master ordered that he and his wife and his children and all that he had be sold to repay the debt.
>
> "The servant fell on his knees before him. 'Be patient with me,' he begged, 'and I will pay back everything.' The servant's master took pity on him, canceled the debt and let him go.
>
> "But when that servant went out, he found one of his fellow servants who owed him a hundred denarii. He grabbed him and began

to choke him. 'Pay back what you owe me!' he demanded.

"His fellow servant fell to his knees and begged him, 'Be patient with me, and I will pay you back.'

"But he refused. Instead, he went off and had the man thrown into prison until he could pay the debt. When the other servants saw what had happened, they were greatly distressed and went and told their master everything that had happened.

"Then the master called the servant in. 'You wicked servant,' he said, 'I canceled all that debt of yours because you begged me to. Shouldn't you have had mercy on your fellow servant just as I had on you?' In anger his master turned him over to the jailers to be tortured, until he should pay back all he owed.

"This is how my heavenly Father will treat each of you unless you forgive your brother from your heart."

MATTHEW 18:21–35

I don't think there are any more chilling words in the entire Bible than in the last line of that passage. If we don't forgive each other, God will treat us as the master treated the unforgiving servant. The message is this: It's impossible to receive forgiveness from God unless we have first given it to others. And if we don't receive forgiveness from God, we are bound for hell.

## WINE MIXED WITH GALL

Forgiveness is a life-and-death decision. If we choose against it, we doom ourselves to hell. Not even God can save us from an unforgiving heart.

But when we push away the possibility of

unforgiveness, we show that our heart is full of grace. This is illustrated in the Gospels. When the Romans were preparing to hang Jesus on the cross, they offered him something to drink:

> They came to a place called Golgotha (which means The Place of the Skull). There they offered Jesus wine to drink, mixed with gall; but after tasting it, he refused to drink it.
> —MATTHEW 27:33–34

This passage tells us something more than the fact that Jesus didn't want a drink. It tells us He was unwilling to accept the bitterness that could have taken hold of any normal person's heart as they were being led to die. Gall was a bitter drink. (See Deuteronomy 32:32.)

*Gall* represents unforgiveness. The world is made of two types of people: those who drink the wine with gall—who get even, whose life is based on revenge—and those who refuse to drink the wine with gall.

Everyone gets handed a cup of gall at some point. Life delivers it on a daily basis—a loved one dies; a friend hurts us, breaks off a relationship or unfairly criticizes us; a coworker goes behind our back or a boss wrongly accuses us. The question is, Do you drink the gall? When you taste the gall of unforgiveness, do you gulp it down to the last drop? Or do you push it away?

A woman was bitten by a rabid dog in the days before there was a cure for rabies. When she found out she was going to die she began quickly writing down names. Someone asked whose names they were, and she responded,

"The names of the people I'm going to bite before I die!"

IT'S IMPOSSIBLE TO
RECEIVE FORGIVENESS
FROM GOD UNLESS WE
HAVE FIRST GIVEN IT TO OTHERS.

Something in the nature of man is willing to drink the gall, to hold a grudge. I read a sad but true story about two men named Tim and Don who lived in Sacramento. One day, both men were on the highway with their families. Tim had just taken his family to a birthday brunch for his wife. Don was going to repair his son's motorized scooter and then head to the shooting range for target practice.

That is, until Don realized he'd taken a wrong exit and quickly swerved back onto the highway—right in front of Tim, who had to hit the brakes.

Tim was angry. He pulled up next to Don, and they began to shout at each other. It all could have ended there, but both men happened to get off at the same exit; while they waited for the light to change they got out to confront each other. As they walked toward each other they yelled, and Don pulled out his gun. Face to face, Tim made a grab for the gun or took a swing at Don, and the gun went off, putting a bullet through Tim's head.

He was dead.

Don was arrested for manslaughter, spent a night in the county jail and was released on bond. A few days later, he placed a call from his cell phone to a 911 dispatcher, telling her he was on his way to that same exit ramp to "serve justice" on himself. Their recorded conversation went like this:

| | |
|---|---|
| Don: | "I just asked God for His forgiveness." |
| Dispatcher: | "He will. He will." |
| Don: | "He won't." |

Don climbed out of his car, sat down at the spot where Tim had been killed and took his own life.[1]

Just think of what could have happened if forgiveness had been injected into that situation.

Tim could have waved happily and let Don back on the highway...

The men could have shaken hands at the off-ramp and apologized for being hot-headed...

Even after Tim was dead, Don could have found a way to forgive himself.

But both men decided to drink the gall of unforgiveness, and they both paid the ultimate price.

## SPITTING OUT THE GALL

Life handed gall to the prophet Daniel, but he was unwilling to drink it. Daniel saw his people taken captive and his parents killed. He became a slave, and they changed his name and may have even made him a eunuch. Life handed him barrels full of gall, but Daniel refused it. He became a high-ranking servant to the king. When he entered the king's presence he could have said, "Die, you dirty dog," but he said,

"May the king live forever."

He didn't give himself the luxury of drinking gall. The one thing Daniel's captors couldn't do was to make him bitter.

Joseph, son of Jacob, was handed several years' worth of gall. He was sold into slavery by his brothers and unfairly imprisoned by Potiphar after being unjustly accused by Potiphar's wife.

Yet he told his brothers, "You intended to harm me, but God intended it for good" (Gen. 50:20). If I had been in his shoes I might have said, "I hope you learned your lesson. Now I'm the king, and I can starve you." But Joseph learned to spit out the gall.

How many times have you drunk the gall and watched that bitterness fill you? Have you seen how it corrupts you inside and out, shades your motives, steals your peace?

Some people suffer in relationships all their lives because a mom or a dad mistreated them. Gall defiles every aspect of existence. What makes it worse is when people feel they have a righteous reason to feel mistreated and believe God is on their side. God can't change your resolve to be bitter. But it's not His will that you keep drinking the gall. Maybe you drank it in the past, not knowing what it was. Now is your chance to be like the wine tasters who spit it out!

When you drink gall, it's all you have to give away. Unless we give forgiveness, we won't get into heaven, nor will we experience forgiveness from others or ourselves.

I've written about the tough times Marja and I

went through early in our marriage. I remember when we were honeymooning in the Philippines right after our wedding. We had been married all of four days and had been bickering terribly. I was preaching our way around the world, combining a ministry schedule with our special time together, and it was a strain on both of us.

VICTORY IS NOT JUST
ABOUT FORGIVING—BUT
HANDING GLORY TO THE
PERSON WHO GAVE YOU GALL.

On the fourth day as we sat in a room in the Philippines, Marja was so homesick. She wanted to go back to Sweden, and I was about ready to send her. Then the old missionary we were visiting showed up and could see we'd been arguing. He asked what was wrong, and I told him, "I've forgiven and forgiven that woman, and I can't do it again!"

He said something I'll never forget: "You'll be forgiving this woman for the rest of your life," he said. "And Marja, you'll be forgiving him. You don't have the luxury of not forgiving anymore."

Those words sank like an arrow into my heart! I didn't learn the entire lesson then, but I've learned it through the years: It's possible to heal as fast as you're wounded. It's possible, as Jesus demonstrated, to shove the gall away without taking a drink. It doesn't matter if the person asks for forgiveness. Your victory is not tied to what they do, but how you react. That way you're never a victim. You're not waiting for them to say the magic words.

I have also found that sooner or later the one who handed you the wine mixed with gall will need you for healing. Victory is not just about forgiving—but handing glory to the person who gave you gall. When you can forgive and help mend the heart of the person who wounded you, you have mastered your situation.

## SWEET WATERS

Another illustration of this is the biblical portrait of two towns, Elim and Marah. Marah was a place of bitter water, but the waters at Elim were sweet. The children of Israel visited Marah, then moved on to Elim.

> And when they came to Marah, they could not drink of the waters of Marah, for they were bitter...
> —EXODUS 15:23, KJV

> And they came to Elim, where were twelve wells of water, and threescore and ten palm trees: and they encamped there by the waters.
> —EXODUS 15:27, KJV

Marah is a symbol of a place of unforgiveness. Why would anyone want to stay there? The waters are bitter, setting your teeth on edge. The bitterness can seep into your family life, business and friendships.

The good news is this: Elim was just seven miles away from Marah, less than a day's journey. That tells us we can leave the bitter waters for the sweet waters anytime we want.

By the same token, Marah is only seven miles from Elim, and some people return to the bitter springs even after tasting the sweet ones.

There was a lady in my church in Davenport, Iowa who was perhaps the single spark that caused revival in that city. She had only been saved for a while, but one day she came to me crying and said, "I don't know if it's all right with you, but I've been knocking on every door to invite my neighbors to church." I told her that was absolutely all right with me!

Her house had been on the market for a year but hadn't sold. We prayed about it, and that week it sold. She gave the money to buy a bus so we could start a bus ministry.

This woman kept winning people to the Lord, and so the rest of the congregation began to follow her lead. Literally, she would bring hundreds of people a week to church, and we bought more buses. She was a prayer warrior, a New Testament Christian, on fire and totally sold out to God.

But one day a superspiritual saint told her that all the outreach and soulwinning she was doing was being done in her flesh. I was furious when I heard that, and the bitterness began to set in no matter how I tried to resolve the situation. This inspirational, soulwinning woman who had helped bring revival to Davenport returned to Marah and drank from the bitter spring. You could see it in her face. She went from being the most productive to being the most critical and unloving person. Today I don't even know if she is following Christ. She went from Elim to Marah in a heartbeat, and as far as I know she hasn't returned.

I admit, I too have lived in Marah at times. I'm tempted every day to visit the bitter springs. It's always a battle to stay sweet even when things around you go sour. But it's a battle worth fighting, because forgiveness is the only way out of the bondage of bitterness.

## "What Have You Done for Me Formerly?"

Someone may have wounded you, hurt you, taken an unexpected jab at you. One way to make it easier to forgive is to take the long view. Instead of asking, "What have they done for me lately?" try asking, "What have they done for me formerly?"

IT'S ALWAYS A BATTLE TO STAY
SWEET EVEN WHEN THINGS
AROUND YOU GO SOUR.

One of the best ways to inspire yourself to forgive is to judge people not on their most recent action, but on their whole track record. When you feel slighted or treated unjustly, think of what someone did for you in years gone by. Why base your opinion on only what they did yesterday?

Too-Tall Jones, the famous Dallas Cowboy football player, quit football to take up boxing and was in a prizefight in Phoenix that I attended. The match went five rounds, and toward the end of the last round, Jones' opponent laid a punch on him that knocked Jones out cold. He lay on the canvas, seeing birds, and the referee began to count: "One...two...three...four..."

When he got to five, the bell rang. The round ended, and the referee did a strange thing. He walked over to Jones who was lying there limp, and he lifted Jones' arm and declared him the winner.

Why? Because Jones had won the first four rounds. It didn't matter that his opponent knocked him out in the last few seconds, because Jones had built a lead too strong to be overcome. The bell saved him from suffering a knockout loss.

That's how we should view our relationships with others. Look at the first four rounds, and if something knocks a person out in the fifth, go over and raise their hands and declare them the winner. That friendship has survived.

Are you having a rough time in your marriage? Think of what your husband or wife did for you throughout the years. Remember how you went through the valley of death together, how you laughed together and all the moments you shared. Get perspective. Can a few negative things in recent days really outweigh the positives of a lifetime together?

Most enemies are former friends, but I say, "Once a friend; always a friend." Should I be angry at the soulwinning woman in my Davenport church just because she's angry at me? No. She did so much for the ministry there that I won't forget her goodness. It's not what she did lately, but formerly, that matters.

Leonard was the head deacon at my church in Davenport. He was largely responsible for my coming to that church at all, because when I tried to wriggle out of my promise to take the pastorate, he insisted that I keep my word and be their pastor. I did, and God sent great revival.

Leonard and I went through years of partnership together with the Lord to make that church effective, but one day Leonard came to me and said he'd gotten to church late and other people had taken his seat. He always sat near the back, and this group from a local retirement home had come and filled up the back few rows because they needed quick access to the bathrooms. Leonard insisted that I do something about it and save those seats for him the following week. I told him the church had no saved seats. His ears got red, and he started to bluster. That precious brother who fought to bring me to Davenport threatened to quit the church.

LOOK AT THE FIRST
FOUR ROUNDS, AND
IF SOMETHING KNOCKS
A PERSON OUT IN THE FIFTH,
GO OVER AND RAISE THEIR HANDS
AND DECLARE THEM THE WINNER.

Do I hold a grudge against Leonard? How could I? Without him I would never have gone to Davenport. I may not have made it to Phoenix. He hasn't done much for me lately, but

that's not what matters. What matters is what he
did for me formerly.

## RUN OUT OF TOWN

Brother Hutchings was a deacon in my father's
church when I was a little boy. He was saved
under my dad's ministry. He and his wife were
firebrands for God, but one day they got mad at
my dad. As a result my dad became discouraged
and feared he had lost the support of the church.
Outside of the will of God, Dad stood in the
pulpit and said that if he got four votes against
him in that church of five hundred, he was going
to quit and move to Texas.

They took a vote, and he got four or five
against him, so he kept his word and moved us
to Texas. I was five years old, and I still
remember that he was the most miserable man
I've ever seen.

Two years later, Brother Hutchings and the
deacon board came to Texas, asked Dad for forgiveness and invited him back to the church. We
came back, and God blessed the church. One day
Dad was out of town, so he invited the YMCA
gospel team to put on a program at church
during his absence. The paper did a write-up
about the YMCA gospel team, reporting that it
was coming to town to speak at Dad's church,
but the team would first go to the local YMCA to
play handball, swim and play pool.

When the deacons heard that the team was
going to play pool, they called a meeting and
canceled the team's appearance. Why? Because

they didn't want pool players in the church! When my dad returned and heard what had happened, he and the deacons got into a serious argument. The deacons decided to kick him out.

I was there the day Dad went out the side door of the church because Brother Hutchings was threatening to whip him when he came out the back door. My dad could have whipped him, but he was too nice to do it. As Dad went out the side door, I went out the back door to challenge Brother Hutchings, and I heard him talking about "whipping the preacher."

I was mad! I stuck my head out that door and said, "That preacher could whip you real good!" Sister Hutchings took her purse and hurled it at me! I ducked, and it missed me.

Do I hold a grudge against Brother and Sister Hutchings? No. In fact, he's still my favorite deacon, though he never spoke to me again. You see, before that, Brother Hutchings had helped me out of a jam. One day in the parsonage I left a cardboard jack-o-lantern burning. To this day I think I blew out the candle, but I can't be certain. We were in church when we heard the fire alarm blaring and the fire truck rumbling down the road. We looked out the window and saw the parsonage on fire. We rushed up, and the neighbor boy kept saying, "I told him to blow out the jack-o-lantern!"

I could have wrung his neck! The firemen put the fire out and told my parents it could have been caused by faulty wiring or by the jack-o-lantern. That's when Brother Hutchings stepped forward. "It was the wiring," he said. "It's always been bad. This is an old house."

I had never loved a deacon like I did then! When I think of Brother Hutchings, I think of what he did for me and my family formerly, not lately, and I still count him a friend.

There was a man in my church in Phoenix who was a dear friend. I loved him and his family. We would go out to dinner, and I would counsel them. He became one of the most generous givers to the church and helped to make our present facility possible. Then one day he broke off our friendship and wounded my heart.

Did I write him off? No. In fact, every year I write him a card to thank him for his contribution to my ministry and the church.

## LIFTING THE HANDS OF FRIENDS

As Christians, we should emulate the referee in that boxing match. Instead of counting our friends out, we should raise their hands and, in forgiveness, declare them our friends no matter what mistakes any of us have made recently.

I'm proud to raise the hands of people like Jim Bakker. For years he invited me to preach on the *PTL Club*. He got knocked out by the devil in the last round, but I'm glad I was one who took his arm after the bell rang and said, "Get up. You won. There's another fight to be fought."

You have to decide: Are you going to be one who forgives or one who holds grudges? Will you push away the gall immediately, or will you taste it and swallow it? Will you stay by the bitter waters of Marah or graduate to the sweet waters of Elim?

When you forgive, you:

- Receive forgiveness from others.
- More readily forgive yourself.
- Receive forgiveness from God.

Let this magnificent, unlimited flow of kingdom grace start with you!

# ELEVEN

# THE GREAT DISCOVERY

W e have seen how giving away brings blessings back to us. But what is a blessing? What does the Bible mean when it says we will be blessed or happy when we give?

Some Christians say all God's blessings are spiritual, such as peace, joy and love. That may be true, but it's not the whole picture.

Some say God's blessings are material and include great wealth. They think Christians should drive around in expensive cars and have mansions for houses. That may be true to an extent, but it doesn't fully define *blessing*.

I have wrestled with the question of what a blessing is for a lifetime and have held different opinions through the years. Early on I subscribed to the view prevalent in Pentecostal circles that God's blessings were purely spiritual, and I rejected the "faith" preaching that said God's blessings were material wealth. My peers and elders said that view corrupted good doctrine.

Over time I realized I was wrong. I had rejected the faith preachers too quickly, Now I know that much of what they say is true. God does want to bless us with wealth, although I am still uneasy when someone puts the emphasis on lavish personal luxury.

## TO ME, A BLESSING IS SOMETHING I ENJOY BY GIVING IT AWAY.

I'm now at a place where I see blessings as multifaceted. Yes, God blesses Christians with wealth and influence, but to me the biggest blessing is being on God's team, working with Him and allowing Him to put tools and resources in my hands so I can use them to change lives.

To me, *a blessing* is something I enjoy by giving it away.

### PREPARE YOUR HEART

Sometimes I wonder how prepared people are to receive blessings from God. To really appreciate blessings, you have to possess a gratitude for what you already have. The only way to appreciate the King-sized blessings of God is to be grateful for the "little" blessings you already have.

- Do you have breath? Praise God!
- Do you have a bed and an enclosed, secure place to sleep? To most people in the world, those things only occur in dreams.
- Can you look forward to a long life because

of modern medicine and cleanliness?

- Do you have all your limbs?
- Does your mind understand the words on this page?
- Are your eyes working?
- Do you have shoes to wear?

I walk through life profoundly grateful for what God has given me, even very small things. It's not an attitude I have to force.

Every time I have a meal or a snack I automatically think of the 99 percent of people in the world who not once in their lives enjoy a meal as good as I eat three times a day. I literally eat like a king—and so do you. I don't have to forage or hunt for food. I simply walk into a restaurant or into my own dining room and the food has been prepared. I sit and eat, not worrying if this will be my last meal for a few days or if it will make me sick.

And when I think of these things, I thank God for His blessings.

When I get dressed or change clothes, my heart is filled with emotion at the thought of how blessed I am to have a closet full of clothes for all seasons. Most people in the world have one or two outfits they wear every day for years. In America, a shirt is considered dirty after one use. I am grateful for the blessing of clothes.

When I read a magazine or book, or watch an educational television program, I think of how few people on earth get the kind of education Americans get. We have access to a deluge of information and knowledge. We are constantly learning. I am grateful for the ability to learn and acquire knowledge.

That's what I mean by preparing your heart to receive blessings. Before you can appreciate the blessing of big things, you have to relish the blessing of "little" things. Don't go about life glibly. Everything you have has been given to you by God. It's all a blessing. How much more blessed can we get?

## EARLY BLESSINGS

Every Sunday before church I wake up early, as early as 4 A.M. sometimes, to prepare my heart. I tell myself, "This morning I get to preach at one of the largest churches in America. I get to be in four services where people will be saved and filled with the Holy Spirit. Never in my wildest dreams would I have thought this possible. I get to go to a church that influences thousands, a church that draws people from around the country. Am I going to treat that lightly? No! This is the church I dreamed of."

With that in mind, I take my role very seriously. I'm not going to wake up late and rush into the sanctuary out of breath. Who knows if the next Billy Graham or president of the United States might come out of my sanctuary? Am I not going to give my best?

What a tragedy it is to be part of the best-fed, best-dressed country in the world and be ungrateful. Even when I answer the phone I quietly ask myself, "What would D. L. Moody or

Charles Spurgeon have done if they had a telephone? How much more could they have accomplished?" As I turn on the radio I think about what Charles Wesley could have done with it. Or Billy Sunday, as animated as he was, what could he have done with the medium of television?

BLESSING
IS A MIND-SET
OF THANKFULNESS
FOR WHAT WE HAVE.

To be blessed is a mind-set that can't be defined in material terms. To you, blessing may be a $100,000-a-year job. To a young boy in Zaire, a blessing may be catching a rabbit to feed his brothers and sisters for a week.

To me, a blessing might be traveling to Europe on the Concorde for my anniversary, which I've always wanted to do. To a girl in Indonesia, it might be escaping a beating.

*Blessing* is a mind-set of thankfulness for what we have. Yes, I believe God has wealth stored up for believers that we are to enjoy and use for kingdom purposes. But I am keenly aware of how easy it is in this culture to take material blessings for granted and to have a sense of entitlement before almighty God.

## GETTING WHAT YOU GIVE

I know for a fact that the quickest way to get what you want is by giving that very thing away. If you want money, give money. Time, give time.

Honor, give honor. Love, give love.

The only time we are entitled to receive His blessings is when we abide in Him. There's a place in God where we can ask for anything and receive it. But the key to finding that place is asking for something that is consistent with His heart. Get inside His mind; get Him inside of you, and then you begin to think as He does. His desires fuse with yours, and you no longer want to ask for Rolls Royces and mansions—you want to ask for food for the hungry. Your desires become like God's desires.

## IT'S IMPOSSIBLE TO GIVE IT ALL AWAY.

I have come to a place that when I ask for something for someone else or for God's kingdom, I'll get it! I never ask for myself because I have enough already. But when I pray for someone else's need, I have the faith that it will happen.

To me, that's the best blessing, the truest honor—being counted worthy to be on God's team, to use my hands, my mind and my voice to carry out His work.

### THE DISCOVERY

After giving everything you have—time, money, energy, love, encouragement, ideas, forgiveness and much more that we haven't discussed—you will come to the most amazing discovery of all. It's a discovery that makes every sacrifice and hardship worthwhile.

It's impossible to give it all away.

You can try and try, but you will never be able to give away everything you have. God will always be right there adding more to your account, whether it's time, money or forgiveness—whatever it is. God is a debtor to no man. After a lifetime of learning how to let go and trust God and to give away what you think is yours, you will ultimately discover that all you had was God's anyway, and that you can never give faster than He can supply. Like the widow's oil that never ran out, the windows of heaven are always open. God is just too big to outgive!

## ONLY THE CROWNED CAN CROWN

There is coming a day when we will get to give something away one last time. I'm not talking about our possessions or our love—or even our lives. Even after we die in the Lord, we'll have one more opportunity to give. We will already be in heaven with Him and with the saints, and we'll have the reward of our labors with us forever. Yet we will still have the chance to give something away.

This last thing we give is eternal. It will be the sum of all that we've done on earth, the symbol of our life's work. It will be something beautiful, so beautiful that eyes and imaginations can't conceive of it right now. It will be lovely, awe-inspiring and worth more than everything in the world put together.

That something is a crown. Someday you and I will wear crowns, like heavenly royalty. Paul wrote:

> Everyone who competes in the games goes into strict training. They do it to get a crown that will not last; but we do it to get a crown that will last forever.
>
> —1 CORINTHIANS 9:25

And again:

> Now there is in store for me the crown of righteousness, which the Lord, the righteous Judge, will award to me on that day—and not only to me, but also to all who have longed for his appearing.
>
> —2 TIMOTHY 4:8

James, the Lord's brother, wrote:

> Blessed is the man who perseveres under trial, because when he has stood the test, he will receive the crown of life that God has promised to those who love him.
>
> —JAMES 1:12

And Peter, the leader of the Jerusalem church and the foremost among the disciples, wrote:

> And when the Chief Shepherd appears, you will receive the crown of glory that will never fade away.
>
> —1 PETER 5:4

When Jesus appeared to John, the writer of Revelation, He confirmed this, saying:

> I am coming soon. Hold on to what you have, so that no one will take your crown.
>
> —REVELATION 3:11

A crown is one of the possessions the Bible says we will have in heaven. The old saying goes, "You can't take it with you." But in a sense, you can. Our crown will be the representation of our good deeds, our endurance in struggle, our faithfulness, our love for Jesus. All that we've done on earth will be summed up in our heavenly headwear.

And yet, what do we do with these crowns once we receive them? Stare at them all day in the mirror? Walk around the streets of gold letting other people notice how ornate our crown is?

It's better than that. After all our struggle and endurance through life, we get to give away our final reward:

> The twenty-four elders fall down before him who sits on the throne, and worship him who lives for ever and ever. They *lay their crowns before the throne* and say: "You are worthy, our Lord and God, to receive glory and honor and power, for you created all things, and by your will they were created and have their being."
> —REVELATION 4:10–11,
> EMPHASIS ADDED

What a wonderful, fitting end to this life! We won't get to heaven and hoard our pile of jewels and riches, the reward for our earthly labor. No, we'll gladly toss our crowns at the feet of Jesus, who makes it possible for us to live forever with Him. That's worth more than a million crowns!

## GAINING A CROWN

But we won't have crowns to throw at His feet until we ourselves are crowned; Jesus is not the King of subjects, but the King of kings. We will be kings under Him, and that's why we will have crowns. Crowns are the uniform of rulers, not

the ruled...of owners and masters, not slaves...
of kings, not subjects.

Where do these crowns come from? How do
we graduate to being kings from mere humans?
The scriptures we just looked at give some clues.
There is the crown of suffering, of longing, of
endurance. I believe there are many thousands of
ways to earn a crown. I believe there is a crown
of soulwinning, righteousness, joy, a crown for
feeding the hungry, caring for orphans and
widows, a crown for martyrs and prayer warriors,
encouragers and financial givers.

## WHAT ARE WE DOING
## NOW THAT'S CROWN-WORTHY?

But also I believe this: You won't get a crown
until you struggle through, persevere and con-
quer something. That's what life is about.

So it's good to ask ourselves, *What will we
throw at Jesus' feet on that day? What crowns will
we have to offer? What are we doing now that's
crown-worthy?*

You don't want to be like the child at the
birthday party who forgot to bring a present.
You'll want to join in with the greatest celebration of all, but the planning for that celebration
starts now as you earn a crown that you can give
away.

### FOLLOWING THE GLEAM

In this book we've talked about giving things
away, which is a way of working toward that
heavenly crown. We don't want to be swayed or

distracted from that goal. A good way of staying focused on the crown is by finding a cause and giving your life to it.

The disciples gave their lives to spreading the gospel. Other people from history have found worthy causes, too. Martin Luther wanted to throw off the oppression of the Catholic church and reintroduce people to God's grace.

In the 1800s, many people in America devoted themselves to getting rid of slavery.

Many people today devote themselves to the struggle for education, nutrition, human rights and freedom of religion. Others devote themselves to writing music, books or stories. Others devote themselves to raising children in a godly way.

I call it *following the gleam.* Whatever puts a gleam in your eye, a sparkle in your personality, that is worth following.

I've tried to follow the gleam to stir up pastors across America to build soulwinning churches. That's been my passion. What's yours? Have you thought about it?

Everyone has a unique gleam to follow. I think of my wife, who raised three children whom I consider my greatest reward. She could have complained about her station in life or accused me of being away too often, coming home tired, having too many responsibilities. But she did none of those things. Instead she followed the gleam to raise our family and lift my burdens when they needed lifting. She makes the time we have together so wonderful that I want to cancel everything else and stay with her! And I believe her devotion makes her a co-owner of the crown I will receive for all the work I've done. She deserves as much thanks for every soul saved in my ministry as I do. She could have griped, but she gave. She followed the gleam, and one day that gleam will lead her to the crown that is her reward.

## WHAT GLEAM ARE YOU FOLLOWING TO YOUR DESTINY?

I used to follow the gleam of living on a golf course in Flagstaff; I even bought property there. It was much cooler in Flagstaff than Phoenix, and my plan was to drive up Friday afternoon, my day off, and come back Saturday evening in time for church in Phoenix in Sunday. But as God began to put the Dream Center vision in our hearts, I realized I would have to trade one gleam for another, and I sold the property just as I was ready to build.

But God has given us a much better thing. We have a vibrant ministry, busy schedules and work to accomplish. My wife and I bought an apartment in a high-rise building in downtown Los Angeles, where we will live someday. We like that apartment better than we would have liked living on the golf course in Flagstaff, I'm sure. We gave up one gleam, but God gave us a better one!

Following the gleam can mean giving up certain things. But the crown at the end of the race is worth it.

What are you doing to earn a crown? What gleam are you following to your destiny? Are you driven by purpose, or are you distracted from the prize?

As I get older I realize I'm getting nearer to crowning time. When I was younger I traveled as much as I pleased and made big plans for the future. Now I have to be more selective about where I go because time is so valuable; when men talk about the great things they'll be doing twenty years from now I quietly wonder if I'll be here.

When I give my last sermon from the pulpit in Phoenix...when I wrap up the last Wednesday night Bible study...when I write my last book and preach my last conference and host my last pastor's conference...I want to be able to say, as Paul did, that I have endured much—scourges, shipwrecks, despair, battles, thirst and hunger, but I was not disobedient to the heavenly vision (Acts 26:19). I followed the gleam. I gave as much as I had for the crown that awaits me.

One day I'll be with the Lord in heaven, and whatever crowns I have earned I will joyfully throw at His feet. Ultimately, that's the destination of everything we give away. It comes from Him and will return to Him, with a host of saints to testify to the goodness of God.

A God who gave His life for us, and who teaches us to give.

# CONCLUSION

This book has talked a lot about giving, but there is still one question that remains. Why does God ask us to give? After all, He owns everything. Why doesn't He supply the food needs, the shelter needs, the encouragement, the love? Why does He ask us to do it?

I think it's because He wants to develop His character in us. He wants us to learn how the kingdom works. Giving is meant to change us, to shape us, to chisel away those parts of us that don't look like God.

There's another reason. When you become a giver, your treasure is invested in other people and in heaven. The Bible says that where your treasure is, there your heart will be. When we give, we make a value judgment about where to put our treasure.

I often drive around our church campus just to see if anything has changed. I sometimes think that I could even notice if a blade of grass or a bush looked different from one day to another. I walk through our buildings and many wings. I check out the fleet of buses. Why? Because I am personally invested in the church. My labor has gone into it. My money has even bought some of those buses. I am invested in the place and the people it serves—and that bonds me to them. Giving is God's way of drawing the body of Christ closer together.

How about you? Have you taken these lessons to heart? Jesus said the wise man would act on what He preached. The foolish man would only listen. If you are the one person in a thousand who listens and acts on this, you will have unleashed the wonderful powers of heaven. You will live a life written about in tomorrow's history books.

Maybe you are that one.

## GIVING IS GOD'S WAY OF DRAWING THE BODY OF CHRIST CLOSER TOGETHER.

When I preach at other churches I often preach on the multiplication miracle. To conclude the service, I call people forward for prayer and hand each of them a palm full of mustard seeds and then pray that the seeds will represent growth. Those times of prayer are so powerful that they become benchmarks these men and women use to measure their effectiveness and passion in the years to come. Sometimes they put the seeds in cellophane packages to remind them.

But whenever I preach at a conference or church I always start with the same prayer. It doesn't matter if there are a hundred or a thousand people present. I pray that God would give me one person who would be inspired. One person for whom I could touch the *believing button.* One person who would make a difference, build a soulwinning church, win their neighbors to the Lord or build a world-changing ministry. Then my trip wouldn't be in vain. I go on these preaching expeditions looking for one person. If I get five, that's a bonus, but I'm really concerned only with getting one, because one person truly inspired can change the world.

A man named John Maxwell came to our pastor's school some years back. He was pastoring a church and felt he and his church needed more motivation. One night during our conference he watched the parade of ministries cross the platform. Later in the week he and the rest of the pastors got on buses after our Sunday afternoon session and went into the Phoenix neighborhoods to bring people to church—a standard part of our conference and a way of teaching the pastors by having them participate in the ministry. We give them two and a half hours to fill their buses and bring people back. Then the pastors sit with them through the service and walk with them to the altar when they get saved.

Maxwell was so stirred that he stayed at the church all night and asked for a room where he and his associate pastors could pray. It was at that conference that his church turned around and birthed a new passion to reach people for God. He is the most effective teacher of leadership skills in the evangelical church today, and an author and speaker much in demand.

One night a man named Leo Godzich, a former journalist, came to a service at Phoenix First and sat on the third row with his wife. He had been attending our church for a while, but he felt something stirring within him to do more.

I did an illustrated sermon that night. I had two trees on the platform, and I tried to get them to bear fruit. I fertilized them and pruned them, and when one of them wouldn't bear fruit, I took out a chain saw and cut it down—right there on the platform. My point was that no matter what we've done, if we stop winning souls God has a right to cut us down—even the pastor.

> ONE PERSON
> TRULY INSPIRED CAN
> CHANGE THE WORLD.

Leo's life was turned around that night. He felt challenged to start a marriage ministry called NAME—the National Association of Marriage Enhancement. Today he hosts conferences around the nation and is doing great work to strengthen marriages. The value of his work to this and future generations of intact families can hardly be measured. I never realized that Leo was the one person I was preaching to that night. Today he's an associate pastor at our church.

In the same way, this book is really for one person. If I get five or ten or a hundred, that's a bonus. But if all the printing and writing and editing costs result in one person who grasps on to these principles, gives his or her life away and changes the world, the investment will be well worth it.

Again I say, maybe it's you.

# NOTES

FOREWORD

1. This foreword, written by Mark Knoles, was written as a sub-
   mission to Your True Hero, and subsequently posted on the
   Internet on Wednesday, September 05, 2001, at the following
   site: www.yourtruehero.org/content/hero/view_hero.asp?29010.

CHAPTER 1: A NEW PARADIGM

1. Laurie Goodstein, "Praised by Bush, a Church Center From
   the Streets," *New York Times* (February 18, 2001): section 1,
   page 28.
2. Source obtained from the Internet: "Mother Teresa of
   Calcutta," a biography available at www.judithcorsino.
   com/teresa1.htm.

CHAPTER 4: THE MOST IMPORTANT THING YOU OWN

1. Author unknown.

CHAPTER 5: GIVING MONEY

1. Source obtained from the Internet: This story can be found at
   http://www.cnn.com/2000/STYLE/design/
   07/07/trendy.tombs.ap/.

2. Ibid.

3. Source obtained from the Internet: Biography of Oseola McCarty, www.starkville.k12.ms/us/mswm/MSWriters AndMusicians/writers/OMcCarty.html.

## CHAPTER 6: BOUNDLESS ENERGY

1. Tommy Barnett, *Adventure Yourself* (Lake Mary, FL: Charisma House, 2000), 5–16.

## CHAPTER 7: HOW TO HAVE UNLIMITED LOVE

1. From "Paracelsus" by Robert Browning.

2. Author unknown.

3. Adapted from "Label-crazy marketers have got you pegged— 32 new categories make consumers easy sales targets," *USA TODAY* (August 1, 2000): 1B.

## CHAPTER 8: ENCOURAGEMENT

1. All of the above, from Edwin Drake to Elvis Presley, are from "A few poorly chosen words from the past," *USA Today* (November 23, 1999): 5D.

2. The preceding anecdotal stories can be found on the Internet at Entrepreneur.com, Inc., © 2000.

## CHAPTER 9: IDEAS

1. Obtained from the Internet, Entrepreneur.com, Inc., copyright © 2000.

2. "Clifton Hillegass; Built CliffsNotes Into Multimillion-Dollar Business, " *Los Angeles Times* (May 7, 2001): B11.

## CHAPTER 10: FORGIVENESS

1. Peter H. King, "A Moment of Road Rage Changes Lives Forever," *Los Angeles Times* (May 27, 2001): B1.

**If you enjoyed *Hidden Power*, here are some other titles from Charisma House that we think will minister to you...**

*Adventure Yourself*
Tommy Barnett
ISBN: 0-88419-665-8
Retail Price: $12.99

God wants you to pursue His dreams for you—dreams that are bigger than you and your life, dreams that will lift you up beyond yourself to reach others and change their lives. Tommy Barnett shares how God has tailored an unparalleled adventure just for you. He created and fashioned you for such a time as this.

*The Leading Edge*
Jack Hayford
ISBN: 0-88419-757-3
Retail Price: $17.99

The *Leading Edge* contains twenty-four power-packed messages from Jack Hayford's best columns written for *Ministries Today*, with additional information and suggestions. Take an in-depth look at his leadership persona and identify rock-solid leadership skills that can help shape an individual into a great leader.

*Nevertheless*
Mark Rutland
ISBN: 0-88419-847-2
Retail Price: $9.99

With one unassuming word, Jesus freed us and revealed the love of God. Jesus captured the awesome power of this word in the Garden of Gethsemane. Jesus prayed, and heaven and earth rejoiced. If you want to confuse the enemy—say *Nevertheless*. Should terrible events threaten to overwhelm you and rip at the foundations of your soul, remember you still have an answer...*Nevertheless*.

To pick up a copy of any of these titles, contact your local Christian bookstore or order online at www.charismawarehouse.com.